Kate Duval Hughes

The fair maid of Connaught

And other tales for Catholic youth

Kate Duval Hughes

The fair maid of Connaught
And other tales for Catholic youth

ISBN/EAN: 9783741197628

Manufactured in Europe, USA, Canada, Australia, Japa

Cover: Foto ©Andreas Hilbeck / pixelio.de

Manufactured and distributed by brebook publishing software (www.brebook.com)

Kate Duval Hughes

The fair maid of Connaught

THE
Fair Maid of Connaught

AND

OTHER TALES

FOR

CATHOLIC YOUTH.

BY

KATE DUVAL HUGHES.

NEW YORK:
P. J. KENEDY
EXCELSIOR CATHOLIC PUBLISHING HOUSE
5 Barclay Street

1889

Entered according to Act of Congress, Jan. 25, 1889, by

KATE DUVAL HUGHES,

In the Office of the Librarian of the Congressional Library, Washington, D. C.

127045

To

His Eminence, Cardinal Gibbons, this little work is most respectfully dedicated with the hope that my faithful efforts may be rewarded by rich fruits from the little buds and blossoms in the great garden of humanity.

Kate Duval Hughes.

I take pleasure in recommending the works of Mrs. Kate Duval Hughes, to be used in families, schools, and libraries for Catholic children and youth. They are good and pure, and while they are made agreeable and entertaining to the reader, there is in each a pointed moral.

J. Card. Gibbons

Balto,
Jany 14, 1889.

TABLE OF CONTENTS.

	Page.
"The Fair Maid of Connaught,"	7
"The Lame Foot,"	61
"Eulalie, or the Little Miser,"	68
"The Good Old Priest & the Snuff Box,"	73
"Lies in Action and Omission,"	78
"Vanity."	82
"Gratitude and Integrity,"	89
"The Faithful Servant,"	108
"Pamela, or the Happy Adoption,"	128
"Punctuality,"	166

The Fair Maid of Connaught.

CHAPTER I.

*"Life is real! Life is earnest!
And the grave is not its goal;
"Dust thou art to dust returneth,"
Was not spoken of the soul."*

Kathleen stood in the doorway. A truly beautiful picture she made; the tall, strong, yet lithe form, draped in the dark blue cloak; the hood falling back from a head whose contour and features were purely classical in their beauty. The limpid whiteness of her complexion, through which the blue veins were traced in all the aristocracy of blue blood, was almost unearthly in its purity; while the carnation bloom on her cheeks had deepened with the healthy exercise she had been taking over the moors; and the dark chestnut hair came rippling down from beneath the hood like the lovely tendrils of some vine. The repose of that sweet face told of one who possessed the kingdom of God within, and the high-toned brow and earnest expression of eye showed some deep resolve—something higher—purer—stronger—better, than the every day struggle—merely to live. She had just returned from one of her missions of love—such love as our Savior preached, when he told us to love our neighbor as ourselves; her daily visit to a poor old bed-ridden woman, almost blind, whose friends all thought that the best thing was to leave her in bed, give her something to eat, and let her alone. Alas! for humanity!—a few old crones it is true would sometimes gather together in her room, smoking, gossiping, and laughing—without much reference to the poor sufferer who was stretched out patiently and quietly on the bed, from which she was never to rise alive. Kathleen's Christian goodness and mercy shone out with an angels light in the sick-room, of this poor, poor creature; she read to her the most comforting and consoling passages of scripture, and on her knees at the bedside said the Rosary with her. "Ah! Mavourneen!" the old woman would often say in trembling voice, laying her withered hand on the silken locks of the Young Girl as she knelt beside her. "May God's best blessing ever rest on ye." And the blessing of the aged, crowned by the threefold blessing of our dear Lord, passed with and upon her through the humble doorway, and she appeared sometimes illuminated, so much glory seemed to shine in her face.

The day was declining, and as she was resting against the door she heard a sweet bird-like voice calling from within—

"Kathleen, is that you?"

It was a voice with a natural trill in it, so emotional was it in all its cadences.

"It is I, Eily— where is my father? I want to speak with him."

"He has gone over to Widow Mc Gleg's to see about the Cow," Eily replied,—

"Come here Ma Vourneen" she continued, "and sit beside me, I have much to tell you, and my heart yearns to unburden itself."— Kathleen turned and entered the inner room where a young girl of sixteen was sitting on a low seat by an open window through which a sweet briar rose and honey-suckle were struggling to enter, as though to caress her.

Kathleen advanced quickly and resting her hand lightly on her head said softly—"Eily— what is it?—any trouble?"

The childish face was upturned to her sister with a tender confiding look—one hand swept back a wealth of hair from a low, fair, candid brow,—while the other grasped her sister's arm—

such hair! it seemed as though a thousand summer's suns had risen and set upon it in all their glory, gently bronzing it with the warmth; it fell down far below her waist in lovely waves and soft curls; the deep blue eyes seemed moist with some tears about to start, and the sweet lips parted, as though to tell some tale of secret grief—at length it broke forth—"Rory has been here to say goodbye—He says his people are down on him, and that he has no luck, and he thinks he'll be off to America"—and the poor little thing broke down completely, and laying her head on Kathleen's shoulder sobbed aloud. Kathleen looked gravely down on the bright childish head that was half buried in the falling tresses.—"Eily, why did you see him again," said Kathleen, " you know our father has forbidden him to come here, and does not wish you to see him, because he does not think he could ever make you happy—he is too wild and unsettled."

" But he has never done any thing really wrong" plead Eily—"and—and—*he loves me so dearly*"—she sobbed.—Alas! for Eily's simple casuistry, by which she tried, as so many other women have done, to prop up their case with the argument of the great love that the other sex bears for them; which so often turns out like the apples on the shores of the Dead Sea—all ashes within.—

If women would only first find out the worth of the subject before they bestow their affection, and then test the strength of their own love, to see if it be strong enough to endure all things, and fight the great "Battle of Life" side by side, there would not be so many failures. But unfortunately, women are so fond of the passive condition of *being loved*, that they very often look no farther—and so, frequently, wake from their dream of happiness, to find themselves shipwrecked on some barren rock—with nothing left to them, but a wild waste.

"*You* are so strong Kathleen," continued Eily, "I am not like you–I know that you will be a nun—every body says so"—and she gave Kathleen a questioning look.

In Kathleen's face came that far-away look it wore so often—as if in her day dreams she was trying to catch a glimpse of some better land—some land of promise—"Yes," she murmered to herself—"I see a hand you cannot see, that beckons me away—I hear a voice you cannot hear, that says I must not stay"—True, there is no charm in the world for me—I shall have no credit in giving it up— the miserable world full of vanity and trouble–full of selfishness and hollowheartedness–Oh! even the rich and gay wordling must feel its emptiness at times, if they stop in the whirl for one moment to reflect—and then the bitter disappointments that they often have to endure, must bring their own sharp sting." " Try and be strong yourself dear Eily, and give up Rory," said Kathleen—"The conscientious effort to detach yourself from such an unworthy object, must bring its own reward. Believe that our dear father must know what is best for his children, whom he has guarded with such precious care, ever since the death of our dear mother."

The girls were motherless, and there was four years difference in their age, Eily being only sixteen, while Kathleen had just passed her twentieth birth-day, and her quiet manner and reflective mind made her seem older still. Their strong old father had taken the place of both parents, and stood in his own home, like some great oak—firm and unbending 'tis true, but sturdy and strong in his intregrity, and undying love for his two daughters.—John Daly was made of that stuff that never bent to the will of another—conscious of his own integrity and rectitude of purpose, he pursued the even tenor of his way, without turning to the right or left, or consulting anyone. His wife Eileen, was very emotional, like Eily, but even more dependent; she clung to her great strong-hearted husband like a timid child, and to see this stern man come out of himself and minister to every little want of a delicate wife, with the gentle kindness of an unselfish woman, was indeed wonderful, and gratifying to all who beheld it.

Eileen Daly was always frail and delicate, but one winter she declined more rapidly, and when March came and the crocusses were just peeping out, she died suddenly one day, leaving her two little girls to their father's care.

He was faithfully devoted to them, but stern and exacting; so they grew up—loving, but fearing him.

CHAPTER II

*"I knew by the smoke that so gracefully curled
 Around the green elms, that a cottage was near;
And I said if there's peace to be found in this world,
 The heart that is humble might hope for it here."*

Elm cottage, on Edgebraugh Farm, so called from the number of beautiful elm trees that surrounded it, was about four miles from Ballinasloe. It was a long, low, rambling house, with large rooms, and many doors and windows, not certainly of the most modern construction, but it had been in the family for many generations, and each member and possessor having found it perfectly comfortable within, and adapted to all their wants, had not cared to enlarge it, or adorn the exterior. It had descended to John Daly from his grand-parents—he was not a man to spend any money foolishly, and as the most thorough comfort always reigned within, he was quite satisfied. It might, with just as much propriety, have been called "Rose Cottage," from the abundance of that lovely flower with which the garden was filled, and all the walls were covered with the clustering rose.

But it matters not—it would have been quite as sweet by any other name, for it was truly the abode of peace and happiness, and that cheerful contentment, which is always the greatest wealth.

A large square porch, supported by pillars made of trees with the branches cut off close, and covered with wood-bine and cluster-roses was the entrance to the "Home."

The first room as you entered was the parlor, a large rather shadowy room, filled with old fashioned furniture, and the walls literally covered with pictures worked in wool—all sacred subjects, and executed by Kathleen and Eily while with the sisters in Balanisloe, and some worked by the mother, and a few by their grandmother—all treasured most carefully. An old-fashioned piano stood in one corner, for both the girls were fond of music, and not only played well, but possessed very sweet voices.

But the inner room was the life and sunshine of the house. Here Eily trilled her sweetest, merriest cadences—Kathleen often joining in with her rich contralto, and the canary trying always to out-do them all. Here the roses climbed into the windows, and all said "Welcome"—all breathed peace and joy.

Here was the home room, where they all assembled, and chatted, lived and loved; and here it was that in the hush of the evening, when the only sounds heard were the distant low of the cattle, and the twittering birds—they gathered together for the evening prayer. Here John Daly offered up his nightly supplication for himself and his children, as he had done all his married life. It was in this room that he always blessed his children before separating for the night.

Beyond this again was a very large kitchen where they took their meals on one side of the room by a long low window, where the roses and honey-suckles climed up together, and interlacing, formed the most beautiful screen that could be imagined. Winny, the only female servant, who had lived with the family over forty years, was generally engaged in the back-ground with the culinary preparations which were performed with that neatness and skill, which were peculiarly her own.

Winnifred Walsh was a character in herself, and so I must devote a little time and space to her definition. She came from Connemara, and her age was very uncertain; judging from the time that she first came to the Daly family—she must have been fifty-five—yet at times, she was so light-hearted, that you could not believe her to be so old. She was rather under-sized, and when you first glanced at her, your impression was, that she was ill-favored; but in spite of a very large mouth, and a dim gray eye—there was such a wonderful goodness of expression—that you looked—wondered—looked again, and liked her.

There was the true stamp of goodness, and in every word she uttered, the ring of the true coin.

Although she could neither read nor write, she was in every sense of the word, the truest christian; bearing about her the visible impress of Christ's love in all her words and actions; so much so, that all respected her, and wished to imitate one, whose life was that of sincere and unaffected piety. Winny had never been known to speak ill of anyone, and whether she heard of weal or woe—it was always "Glory be to God"— throwing up her hands at the same time, as though to praise God for all His acts. "The aisy way is always the best" Winny would say to her children as she called them, and Kathleen and Eily had fewer children's squabbles than usual.—Winny's working attire was peculiar—a dark blue woolen petticoat, with her purple calico tucked up and pinned behind; large list shoes adorned her feet, and a scrupulously white 'kerchief pinned across her bosom. She never wore a cap as is usual with the women of the country-but her hair combed back smooth across her brow and gathered up in a little knot behind; it was brown hair slightly silvered with gray-and was soft and fine as that of an infant—her hands too, although she had done much hard work in her life, were quite slender and shapely. John Daly always said of Winny—"If the shell is not pretty, the kernel is sweet"—and it was so;- she was truly good, and was much cherished and beloved by all the family, and was looked upon not so much in the light of a servant, as a friend of the house-hold.—

I must not forget to introduce one other of John Daly's retainer's, and these two constituted the staff of house servants.

Pat Mc'Gorhen, was Winny's nephew, a lad of eighteen years of age, strong, healthy, good humored, and good hearted. He drove the car, attended to the horses and cows, the garden, and in fact all the jobbing work that was to be done. Tall, and well formed, his face presented an odd mixture of shrewdness and innocence; his large light blue eyes were always wide open, and so was his mouth generally speaking, displaying when he smiled an even row of very white teeth; his nose, which is the most important feature in the human face for bestowing, or taking away strong character of expression, stood out in a straight line from the middle of his face, and I cannot describe it more graphically than to say, that if his course through life was always governed by his nose, that it would be thoroughly straight forward. When any one was speaking to him, he would look most persistently and undeviatingly into one corner of the ceiling, as though trying to solve some geometrical problem there. This was Pat's physiognomy. His heart was in the right place, and as fresh as his face; while like Winny he was honest, true and faithful.

John Daly could have lived in much better style had he chosen to do so; but he did not believe in making a show to please the world. He was contented if his children were comfortable and happy, and he would rather give two or three thousand pounds to help build a church, or endow a convent, than to waste it in any way to gain the applause or admiration of the multitude. His mind was very much exercised, and his heart troubled at the present time, by the miserable influence that Rory O'Hare had gained over the heart of innocent Lily, and he had strictly forbidden him to visit the farm, or Eily to see him.

Rory O'Hare was one of the weakest, most irresolute characters that one could possibly describe; he would have liked to have been something, if only some one could have watched him carefully—nerved him—brought him to the starting point, and kept him there until something was achieved—constantly making good resolves—he was as constantly shifting from them—so that at twenty-six he could only look back upon more than one-third of his life passed in wavering and uncertain steps, that had led him nowhere in particular, and had gained him nothing.

His love for Eily, if you could give it that name, was of the most selfish kind—unable and unwilling to make the least sacrifice for her. John Daly, with his strong good sense, could not brook the idea, for one single instant, of his sweet little innocent, confiding Eily, being shipwrecked in this cruel manner upon such a wretched quicksand as this Rory O'Hare; and he fully resolved to use not only his paternal influence, but authority, to bring her safely anchored in some port, where her comfort and happiness would be secured, and where he could, while living, watch over her with that vigilant eye of tender care, that only a fond parent can exercise.

CHAPTER III.

The Parting.

"*One touch of nature makes the whole world kin.*"

It was an "incense breathing morn" in the sweet and flowery month of June—when Lily prepared for a walk after breakfast.

Three times did she run up to her little bedroom to arrange her dress, and smooth again her luxuriant tresses, which would, in spite of all care, bound about in all the abundance of wealth, rippling up here, and curling down there, until the little one had to laugh, herself, at the determination each lock showed of going its own way. Now, it was to tie her hat ribbons more neatly and coquettishly under her little fat chin—now, to smooth her skirt and arrange her scarf—and lastly, to fasten a few choice rose-buds in her bosom.—Finally as there seemed to be nothing more that could be accomplished in the way of improvement, she descended the stairs, stopping to caress her pet kitten, who looked wonderingly at the unusual amount of affection lavished on her; then hovering over the canary's cage and trilling gently a soft lay, at which the canary shrieked wildly,—hopping madly about from perch to perch, with his head first on one side and then on the other; then meeting Winny, who had been following her all the morning with wistful eyes and anxious brow, she burst into tears.—

"May God direct you to the best my wean," said Winny following her to the door—"God bless you Mavourneen," and the little one was folded in the old woman's arms before she set out.

What a lovely morning it was! The air was redolent with sweets, such as cloy not the senses or satiate the heart. Great nature seemed to open her arms and say—"Here my child, partake of all my rich gifts and enjoy them. I shower my innocent enjoyments on all without preference, that all may live, and love, and delight."- The clear blue vault of Heaven was cloudless, and the air rich with the sweetest odors—purified by the healthfulness of the country.

Eily tripped along lightly with all the buoyancy of youth, with a happy and innocent heart.—

The slight cloud of care, that seemed to have rested for a while over her childish face and gay spirits, was lifted and carried away by the sweetness of the atmosphere, and the rich and varied beauty of the scene.

The grass was as ever in "Erin's Isle," of the brightest, richest green. The hawthorn was out in its full luxuriance—every daisy seemed to lift its head in star-like beauty, to welcome the sweet little one, and the hare-bell shook its tremulous flowers—and all seemed to Eily to ask a mute, yet questioning "Well"?—to which her heart could only answer—still—farewell—on she sped, her feet scarce touching the ground, her bloom deepening, and her eye gathering more earnestness—when a sudden turn in the road brought her to a lane, whose rural beauty was enough to entice any one to seek it, and linger long; where nature seemed to have laid some cunning plan to ornament this spot of sylvan loveliness where in the human heart might love to rest. A perfect avenue was formed of the Elms and Ash trees —whose branches seemed almost to touch above. The soft, rich grass was only disturbed by a little foot-path running through, while each side was bordered with the wild primrose , violets, and hyacinths with all their odorous beauty—till some parts looked like a gay parterre.

With childish glee Eily could not resist stopping at intervals to gather these sweet flowers of which she was so fond, and with that youthful desire to grasp the beautiful and the enjoyment of the hour, while passing down the stream of life—she stopped—gathered—ran on—stopped again, and culled her sweets until she was literally laden with a wreath of nature's choicest gifts, her pockets, arms and hands filled. Running on quickly, she saw before her, at the end of the lane, in front of the hawthorne hedge, Rory O'Hare! There he stood—his hat pulled partly over his eyes—an expression half pleased, half defiant in his face—indolence in his attitude—shifting his position uneasily—glancing at Eily, who ran towards him quickly—holding out her hand frankly—exclaiming—while a blush passed over her ingenuous face—"Oh! Rory! I am so glad to see you once more—though, it must be the last time," she added sorrowfully. He grasped her hand feebly, and held it in his—"Why must it be the last time Eily ? I care more for you than any girl in the world." "Do you?" said Eily, looking away sadly—the thought flashed across her mind, though she scarcely understood it herself—so unwilling are we to believe that which is disagreeable; that perhaps he did not care for anyone—not even herself; it really did look like it. He had never made the slightest exertion to settle himself, to do anything to win her, to make himself deserving of her love, or the respect and confidence of her dear father —a great many thoughts crowded together rapidly in her mind, as she stood there weak and wavering, and looking so utterly irresolute and miserable.

Eily was very young and guileless, but she seemed to grow suddenly many years older in a very short space of time. "What are you going to do Rory?" said Eily quietly. "I don't hardly know," said Rory looking with great uncertainty over the hedge, as though he might find something in the space beyond. Eily was silent—her heart beat quickly—she scarcely thought she ought to be there, as she was now—although it was only to say good-bye; and it must come to an end quickly. She stood there sadly—she had let the flowers fall to the ground, and Rory's hand too—she had let go.

Possibly, she thought that a hand that would give her no support, was not worth keeping—and the devotion that she thought she felt for him was fast flickering, and dying out to the last spark. Still if she had thought it was her duty to stand by such a being, who was not able to be even a half of anything, she would have done so, she was too good, and loyal, and true, to draw back from what she could do consistently and rightly to save anyone; but the commandments were ever in Eily's heart, engraven there, and the one with *promise* above all others, and the thought of her father in all his integrity and goodness—his faithful love, and tender care—made the contrast still more odious. At this moment, when filial love and duty were struggling for the mastery, the temptation was becoming weaker and weaker.

Rory felt painfully Eily's silence, and wished to make one more appeal.

"My people don't do what is right by me Eily"—said he, "and sometimes I think—I should'nt wonder—if I went to America."—"Is not that very far off? said Eily gently—as though he were telling her something out of a book. Eily's geographical knowledge did not extend quite so far, and it seemed to her like going to some great wilderness.—Her hat had fallen off, and she caught it by the ribbons. Her lovely hair fell over her face, and around her shoulders in a wreath of golden waves—the sunbeams seemed to stoop through the slight opening in the trees to kiss the fair brow—her blue muslin dress fluttered in the morning breeze, and the sweet face upturned in its childish wonderment, seemed more angel than mortal, in all its simplicity and innocence.

"It seems to me that you take my going very easy, and don't care how far off it might be." "I cannot help it Rory, and wherever you would do the best, would make me the happiest." "I mind me of girls," said Rory boldly, "who would go with a fellow."

Had a random shot pierced her heart, for one moment she could not have suffered more anguish;—her slight form grew taller and taller, as she drew herself up in her wounded pride and dignity—her face grew paler and paler—till to Rory's frightened gaze she seemed to be a spirit from another world. "Do you—mean—that—Rory?" said Eily in almost a whisper—"Do you mean—"—here sobs and tears choked her utterance.—She stepped back several steps, putting her hands before her, as though to shut out some terrible sight.

Rory had sunk back against the hawthorne hedge—pushed his hat back, and was gazing at her in wild amazement. "I mean," said he, "if we were married and all was right—what else would I mean shure;" still she stepped back and put out her hands before her helplessly.

"Is that the way you say good-bye to a fellow?" said Rory."

She let her hands fall—stood still one moment,

and said softly—"good-bye Rory," turned slowly round, and tottered rather than walked, to the end of the lane. Then resting against a tree, she quietly put on her hat, and stepped out on to the road.

CHAPTER IV.

The summer passed uneventfully, quietly and pleasantly; Eily drooped a little sometimes, but was sustained by Kathleen's brave spirit, and strong will. The autumn was ushered in, with bright sunshiny days, and long lingering twilights, and great preparations were being made throughout the country for the great annual fair, held in Ballinaloe during the first six days of October. The great display of black cattle, horses and sheep was always very fine, but this year it was thought that it would exceed all others; the farmers had been so successful in the raising of their stock.— John Daly's cattle were always considered some of the finest, and he watched for the fair to open with great eagerness, and as he always took his daughters with him, and they were ever the subject of great admiration—of course, his paternal pride was very much gratified.

At last the 1st of October arrived and Kathleen and Eily were donning their best attire. Pat had been currying the horses,—cleaning his boots—soaping his face, and brushing his hair since day-light, interrupted occasionally by Winny's quiet remark, "Why Pat boy! Shure you must think you are going to find somebody at the fair that ye like better than yerself," at which playful sally, Pat would grin, and then scrub away.—At last the car was at the door—the horse was gay with ribbons—while Pat's hat was adorned with a green band and a bunch of shamrock.—John Daly stern and stiff, handed his lovely daughters into the car, and then stepped in himself. Pat touched the horse, and they flew off along a smooth road, and all seemed happy and bright. Eily, it is true, looked slightly pensive and pale, and kept her secret to herself, though she might suffer.— Kathleen's steel colored silk and white hat with a long plume, only served to enhance a beauty so particularly rare and uncommon, while her simple elegance added to her distinguished appearance.

The drive, and the morning air brought the color into Eily's face, and she soon was chatting gaily; her white dress and blue ribbons fluttered in the breeze, and her father looked satisfied and smiled gravely. Kathleen appeared even on the car, as though she were seated on a throne, and this day she seemed to look more queenly than ever. Soon they reached the fair ground, and were mingling with the gay throng who were fast assembling. Cordial greetings met them on every side, for they were much respected and beloved through the country. Eily's face sparkled with happy and innocent enjoyment, while Kathleen's earnest face and grave dignity, only served as a grand contrast.

"Kathleen," said her father, "there is Lord Eversly with Guy Dominick. Don't you remember Guy?" "I do," replied Kathleen, "very well." A bright flush suffused her face, as his name was mentioned. He had offered himself in marriage three years before, and had been rejected; but he had sworn never to forget, and always to love her.—Just then the two men passed; Lord Eversly staring boldly at the beautiful girl. "I say, Guy, who is that beauty? She has a brow that would grace a coronet. By jove! I think I never saw anything so grand even during a London season."

"I suppose not," said Guy. "Kathleen Daly would stand alone in her peerless grace and beauty among a million London belles."

Ha! Guy, "you must have been struck." "Perhaps so," said Guy, quietly; deeper indeed than anyone knew.

"Well! I should not mind having a flirtation with the damsel. She looks like a calla lilly with that white hat and plume. I think I could woo and win her, and spend my time pleasantly."

"You"—said Guy between his teeth,—" you might as well try to pick a star out of the heavens as to win Kathleen Daly, much less trifle with her." "I have wooed gayer girls than that," said Eversly. "I have shot at higher marks, and bagged my game. I say, Guy, you must introduce me."

Guy Dominick's face grew white with suppressed rage, but he did not dare refuse, lest his deep feeling should be seen, and his motives judged mean and contemptible; so they wandered through the crowd until they approached the Daly's and the introduction was over; Guy's distressed face and pleading manner plainly saying, Kathleen, I could not help this.

Lord Eversly bowed and addressed Kathleen with that well-bred, easy assurance, that marked so plainly what his success had been, among his own circles in England, yet when Kathleen returned his bow, in her own stately manner, and quiet grace, and opened wide those dark gray eyes, meeting his impertinent gaze with calm astonishment; he felt for the first time in life, that he had met at last a superior being; something higher, purer, better; something out of his reach, that he could not penetrate, or define, or make the slightest impression upon. In vain did he speak of the weather, and gaze admiringly in her face. In vain did he criticise the cattle, and ask her if she was fond of horses. In vain did he shrug his shoulders and ask her if she had ever been to the races. The same calm, wondering expression met him. The same half-scornful pity played round her mouth. Dignity alone forbidding the utterance of words, whose expression was plainly on her lips.

Never were whiskers and mustache so mercilessly pulled, as his were, in his nervous rage, and being so completly nonplussed in his vain arrogance and conceit. Never were gloves put on and pulled off so often, and in vain did he switch his cane, and wish himself in all sorts of hot places. There was a slight response from the "Calla Lily." She turned her white throat, bowed and looked on in great beauty and silent wonder.

But in the midst of Lord Eversly's helpless despair, the approach of Mr. Daly, with young Thorne, from Athlone, came to his rescue. John Daly having properly introduced Mr. Thorne to his daughters, turned to Lord Eversly to ask him what he thought of the fair.

"Very good," said Lord Eversly nervously. "I am quite pleased. By the by Mr. Daly, I understand that you have some very fine cattle, here, will you show them to me?" "By all means, with pleasure," said Mr. Daly, proud to display what he prized next to his daughters. "Come this way Lord Eversly, and I will show you the finest milch cows on the grounds."

Bowing farewell to Kathleen and her sister, Lord Eversly wandered about with John Daly until they found the spot set apart for his display of cattle. These he showed with a true-hearted farmer's pride, dwelling on each good point with emphasis. They then trotted along to look at the horses, and brought up by the sheep, which were remarkably fine this year. "I'll warrant a good many of these will pass and be sold for Devonshire mutton this year, eh!" said John Daly.

"Do you think so—?" said Lord Eversly smiling grimly—"Perhaps so"—Lord Eversly was absently thinking of the woman who had so shaken him on his pedestal. No Englishman likes to be nonplussed, and it had made him moody and gloomy, and he did not know well what to do with himself. He slipped off at last from Mr. Daly, and wandered about by himself, sticking his hands in his pockets, which is always a great comfort and relief to an Englishman when in trouble of mind, or when making any calculations, or when discomfited in any way. His brow was contracted, and the more he thought, the deeper his hands dived into his pockets. *He did not like the idea* of being *shaken on his pedestal*—and he remembered Guy Dominick's scathing remark:" *You might as well try to pick a star out of the heavens as to try to win Kathleen Daly.*" What right had this young Irishman to make such a remark to *him*—a person of his social standing?—and then what made it more humiliating still was that it did *seem* as though he *had* met with something *out of his reach.* He wished now that he had not wasted his time in running up from Dublin to this confounded fair, where he had encountered such a defeat. It really was sadly mortifying. How could it be possible that after so many successful seasons in London where every beauty seemed to smile upon him, and all the mammas were so cordial and attentive, and all looked and acted as though they would be glad to have him for a son-in-law;—for Lord Eversly's estates were unincumbered, and his title was not from yesterday, but dated from generations back. How could it be possible that this country girl should receive him with such cool indifference, and assume such airs? Yes, it was decidedly airish, and confoundedly stupid, and he "had been shaken on his pedestal;" and the hands came out of his pockets, and began pulling the whiskers again. It was a problem; and Lord Eversly did not possess sufficient mathematical talent to solve it.

CHAPTER V.

Leaving Lord Eversly to solve the problem that had so shaken his British pride, and wounded his self-love; we will return to the two girls and Mr. Thorn.

Michael Thorn belonged to that type of Irish well-to-do farmers, whose pastoral life of Arcadian simplicity and innocency is, perhaps, unequalled at the present day in any other portion of the globe. His ancestors, from one generation to another back, had always been farmers—tilling their own land, and enjoying modest and independant competency crowned by good consciences and light and happy hearts.

He was the third of seven sons, who all lived at home in the old paternal homestead, although two were married, and had families of their own. Yet they were all united in the bond of good fellowship, and that strong and abiding law of

"Kith and Kin" nowhere so beautifully illustrated, and adhered to, as in Erin's Green Isle, and her own faithful people. The "boys," as they were still called, all helped on the farm, and vied with each other in being good to the old people, who were now in declining years, and had given up almost all interest to their children.

They were fine manly specimens of young men, being nearly all six feet in height, and broad shouldered, and deep chested in proportion. But Michael rather excelled them all in his masculine beauty. His stature and fine bearing would have made him a splendid martial commander, had he followed a military career—while his keen intelligence, and natural flow of rhetoric would have enabled him to make a good special pleader in any of the courts, had he been destined to follow the legal profession. But no such restless ambition disturbed the equanimity of his fresh heart and contented mind, and in his ingenuous face you saw only the desire for honest labor and daily bread, a good wife and happy family. The smooth fair brow was not wrinkled by any of the "eating cares of life," and the deep, clear blue eye spoke only of strict integrity and honest worth. His vigorous and manly beauty bore ample testimony to the purity of his life, while his intelligent conversation showed that although his education had been limited, yet he clearly understood all he knew. Kathleen had received him with stately though gracious kindness, and Eily's blushing shyness, only made her appear more lovely in his eyes. They wandered off to seek some refreshments—all on the most cordial and easy footing, as the two families had been old friends for many years. At last Mr. Daly joined them; and after Mr. Thorn had taken Eily to look at a very beautiful pony, Pat was called with the car, and they got ready to return home. "Get in, Thorn, and come home with us to supper; I will send you into town again to-night if you must return." "I fear I must," said Michael, "but I shall like the drive home with you all the same."

The horses sniffed the air, and travelled faster than in coming. They were all tired when they reached home, where Winny had a delightful old-fashioned supper prepared for them, and where they enjoyed some mirth and pleasant conversation before parting for the night.

"Come over soon and see us, Thorn" said Mr. Daly, "we are always glad to see you."

"Thank you, I will."

CHAPTER VI

An old fashioned Wooing

Love is a little fragile flower,
That in the garden of the heart,
Springs up unbidden in an hour.

The flower grows in pensive beauty,
Without a thought or care;
Until its perfume softly rising,
Tells that the flower is there.

Eily's slumbers that night were somewhat disturbed by a vision of manly grace and beauty that flourished about in her dreams, and flitted here and there with her in walks, and in woods, and groves; and only vanished with her waking, to her great disgust and disappointment. She threw open her window to breathe the fresh morning air, and as the sweet roses brushed in and kissed her lips, and shook off the dew drops, and the whole scene lay before her in radiant beauty, she thought again, that life was still, with all its ups and downs, very beautiful, and very enjoyable; and that, perhaps, there was something very bright in store for her; and a great many visions of earthly happiness and comfort, ease and prosperity, and multiplied blessings crowded in upon her mind as she sat down in the early morning sunshine to brush out her lovely and luxuriant hair. She brushed energetically, and the exercise and friction seemed to restore the vigor of the brain, and the tone of her thoughts. She found herself wondering how she could possibly ever have tolerated Rory, and whether it was probable that Michael Thorne would take a fancy to such a shy little thing as herself. With that possibility growing in her mind came such a train of glorious and bright imaginings for the future, that it was long before she had gathered up her tresses and prepared to descend to breakfast.

Kathleen and her father had evidently been having a close and earnest conversation, of which Eily felt, that she had been the subject. It is strange how we sometimes feel these things and in this case it was so. Mr Daly had been speaking very seriously to Kathleen about his wishes on the subject, expressing very earnestly what a satisfaction and comfort it would be to his father's heart if such a good young man as Michael Thorn would take a fancy to his sweet little motherless Eily, and as she entered, the conversation ran thus:—

"And then," continued Mr. Daly, "Thorn has so many sons at home that Michael could live here, and Eily need never leave her own old home. I'm sure she would feel like a fish out of water in any other."

"Yes," continued Kathleen, "that would be nice for dear Eily, and a pleasant comfort to you dear father, to have in your old age, a good son like Michael to lean upon—and then—dear father, I can go to *my* bridal."

"Ah, yes, Cushla Machree, I know very well where your heart is, and I should not have kept you in the world pining so long for your rest, if I had not wished to see Eily settled first. You know you have always taken the mother's place.
"I should liked to have offered the first blossom of my youth to our dear Lord," said Kathleen, sadly. "You will do so," said her father gravely. "The first fresh bloom has never been brushed off by contact with the world. Truly Kathleen Mavourneen you have kept yourself "unspotted from the world." "I hope so, father, my *heart* has never been in it."

Eily's appearance at this moment, all radiant with hopeful smiles and blushes stopped the conversation.

"Kathleen," said Eily, after awhile. "What are you going to do to day? I want you to go to the woods with me."

"Well, Colleen, we'll go," said Kathleen. Accordingly, they set out after breakfast, taking by chance, the road that led to the lane, down which Eily had bidden farewell to her worthless lover. "Not there Kathleen," said Eily. "Not there;" growing pale as she spoke.—Why not Colleen" said Kathleen gravely. "No matter," said Eily. "Come this way;" quickly turning as she spoke, in an opposite direction.—Then they found themselves on the road to Athlone, and before they had gone very far, who should they meet but Michael Thorn, standing before them, unmistakable joy shining in his honest face, when he saw the two sisters advancing toward him. Cordial greetings passed, when Kathleen exclaimed: "If you don't mind, Eily, I will turn round and go on to Ballinasloe, as I wish to visit the Sisters to-day."—They neither of them looked as if they minded it much to be left alone; on the contrary, they seemed so entirely absorbed in each other, much to Kathleen's great amusement. They all turned and took the road to

Ballinasloe, but Eily wearying a little of the high road, and expressing a desire for some beautiful wild flowers in a wood close by—Kathleen told them to ramble about in the woods, and that she would continue her walk to the town alone, and return to dinner.

They wandered on, hand in hand,—Michael with tender care, clearing away every obstacle in her path. The weather was rather warm, a sort of dreamy day, the sunshine glinted in through the branches of the trees, throwing flickering rays across the path, and darting here and there in glancing glee. The birds sang their love songs over head, and the flowers lent all their sweet odors for the passing hour, and this was indeed the atmosphere of love.

In such spots Cupid is always lying in ambush with his quivers; and I have no doubt that on this remarkable occasion, he was at the top of some tree taking sure aim.

Eily darted about with the shy grace of a fawn, gathering flowers, mosses and ferns, as often returning with innocent confidence, and a rising blush, to place again her little white hand in Michael's broad palm. There certainly was in the mute grasp of that honest hand, a world of sparkling and bestowing protection; and Eily felt a decided restful feeling, bringing strength and calm to her young heart, that had lately been troubled by emotions of a most unquiet nature. They wandered on, till they came to a cool, delicious spring which sprang from a rock, around which the ferns and lichens seemed of a richer green.

Eily stooped down in childish glee, and making cups out of the leaves, drank, and made Michael quaff the cool water from one of her newly invented drinking cups.—Michael never grew weary, and Eily's confiding happiness ever on the increase, knew no alloy. A babbling brook arose from the spring, and wandered along through the dark woods, curling and winding about in its silvery beauty—rippling on, and seeming to echo all their low and tender words. At last, after numerous turnings in and out—so happy that they knew no fatigue—Michael selected a lovely spot for Eily to rest awhile; here the brook took a sudden leap over some large rocks, making a sort of small cascade, tumbling down in white foam, and then disappearing for awhile under a large moss-covered stone. Here they rested, and listened to the music of the waters; Michael tenderly placing Eily on a seat of moss, under a wide-spreading alder tree, seated himself beside her. She had taken off her hat and filled it with flowers. She placed it on the ground, and commenced playing with the white foam of the brook, letting the water pass through her fingers laughing merrily.

"Are you tired Eily?" asked Michael.

"No," replied Eily, "I should like to stay here all day, but Kathleen will expect me home to dinner."

"I am always very happy with you Eily," said Michael.

"Are you?" said Eily, looking trustingly into his face.—

"Yes, I am, and I should like to make my happiness sure for life."

"How?" said Eily, stopping her play with the water.

"By asking you one simple question."

"What is that?" she said, looking at him wonderingly.

"It is this," said he taking her little hand in his own, and holding it fast. "*Will you be my own true wife, Eily?*"

The blush rose and covered her face and neck, the eyes drooped, till the brown lashes lay on her rosy cheek. Her bosom heaved with a wild, yet suppressed emotion, and when she raised her eyes to meet his tender gaze, and reply to his repeated question, they were filled with tears, and she answered softly—

"*I would like to be,* Michael."

"Would you Mavourneen? Then you *shall*

be, and that right soon;" and his ardent and impetuous nature had carried him off in imagination to the church, and he was carrying her home, a bride, his own. He sprang to his feet, and catching her by the hands, raised her gently, yet quickly—" Say that again dear Eily, say that once more."

"I have said it once, and forever," said Eily, "and 'tis true."

" Ah! and you will be true dear one, for life? You will never have cause to regret those words, for I'll be good and true to you Eily."

" I know that. I feel it, I believe it, but had you not better speak to my father about it?"

This day I'll settle it. Never fear, Colleen." Then with her little hand resting on his strong arm, and her little feet trying to keep pace with his manly strides, they wandered back again by the side of the babbling brook; but this time, the music of the waters was changed; they sang a sweet low song of satisfied, trusting hearts—of love and peaceful contentment and home. There seemed to be a spring in the ground upon which they trod; the birds sang a louder, merrier lay; the flowers bloomed more brightly; the secret of which was that two loving souls had melted into one and had found a *great happiness.*

CHAPTER VII.

There was but one shadow hovering over Eily's brightened pathway, and that was the thought that Michael ought to know all about Rory O'Hare. With the true instinct of a true woman, she wanted no concealments; she wished to start life with perfect trust and confidence; so that she might know exactly where she stood, and fear no shipwreck. She wondered what Michael did know, or what he had heard; but of this, she could gain no insight; and was groping helplessly about by herself in the dark. She felt that she would be happier and better satisfied if Michael knew that there had been an attachment, but that it was over, and they had parted forever. She felt at last that she would rather tell him herself. It would be much better that he should hear it from her own lips. He could only have heard some of the neighbors gossiping; and not much of that; and it seemed to her ingenuous mind, that it was a first and last paramount duty to tell him the whole story. Having nerved and braced herself up to the point of confidential disclosure, Eily soon found an opportunity of unburdening her mind and heart.

One evening Michael had lingered longer than usual, and Eily had followed him to the gate, to bid one more farewell, when the thought struck her that, perhaps, no more convenient opportunity would offer itself, to make the necessary confession.

They stood by the gate, hand-in-hand, and Michael was telling her that he would be over earlier the next day, and that it would be only two weeks now before the wedding.

"That will be the happiest day of my life," said Michael, "and I hope it will be the same to you Eily."

"I hope so," said Eily, "I feel so—but Michael—I have something to tell you before you go—or to ask you."

"What is it dear?"

"Did you know Rory O'Hare?"

"I did," said Michael—" not very well. He was a worthless fellow, and the family were glad to send him to America—to see if he would better his fortunes there. He was not worth knowing—There was nothing in him."

"No.—I suppose not"—said Eily dreamily—"I heard that he had gone away. Then after a pause she commenced again—

"Did you know that he visited me?"

"Oh, yes; I heard that he was hanging about the home—I supposed it was to see you. Why not Colleen?—You are the prettiest lass in the country—everybody knows that; but I heard that your father forbade him the house."

"That is true," said Eily, quite relieved to find that Michael knew so much, and yet, the hardest part of the task was yet to be done, and she scarcely knew how to word it. An ominous silence fell upon them—neither spoke for a few moments, which seemed very long to poor Eily; the twilight was deepening—Michael had one hand upon the gate-latch, where it had been for the last half hour, but he hated so to go, that the gate remained closed; the other hand clasped Eily's hand, while she played nervously with her apron. She had been looking up at him, but now her glance wandered up, through the trees, and out beyond into the empty space.

"What is the matter, Eily? What are you thinking of; the blushes rose over her brow and throat, but the twilight was deepening, and Michael did not see them.

The moment had come at last—she *must speak*,

a lump was rising in her throat, and her voice trembled.

"Did you ever think Michael, that *I cared* for Rory?—

Michael had been looking down into her eyes, trying to read her thoughts.

"No,"—said Michael firmly, in his deep voice—"I never thought so—I did not think you would waste your liking, on such a worthless fellow."

Here was a dilemma! What should she do now? What could she say? If he had only *thought* that she *had* liked him, and that it was over—the task would have been finished. But now—she would have to find some other way, some other words, and poor Eily was sore oppressed, and in great perplexity. Her little fingers twitched and pulled at her apron still more nervously.

"Would you mind it, Michael, if you thought I *had ever cared* for Rory?" said Eily, her lips quivering—"would you mind it, if I told you I *did* like him—once? Eily breathlessly waited for his answer. "No," exclaimed Michael still more firmly—"I should not mind it—it would not hurt me in the least—You may have had many fancies in your little head—many likings and dislikings, for aught I know—*but they are all past*—You have told me that you loved *me*, and I have believed you, because I know you to be good and true. You have given me your *whole heart* have you not Eily? and we have pledged and plighted our troth, and *that means*, that we must go on *trusting* till the end of life."

The tears that stood in Eily's eyes ran down her cheeks—but they were now tears of joy. The confession was over—she rested trustfully and confidingly on that great manly heart that knew no fear, no doubt.

The twilight had deepened into dark—the quiet stars shone out, and blinked and winked, as much as to say, "It is all right *now*."

One heart felt pressure of the hand,—one more—one last good night,—and the gate opened and swung to on its hinges.—The latch clicked—a slight form hurried up the gravel walk to the porch—the hall door closed—and all was hushed in silence—peace—and night.

CHAPTER VIII.

THE WEDDING.

The home was alive, and astir with the preparations for the wedding, for only a few days now intervened. Winny was up to her eyes and elbows in wedding cake. Pat was uproarious, and seemed disposed to turn summersaults. Kathleen stitched away with unwearying hands on frills and laces, and all sorts of pretty things.

Eily was busy too, but seemed in a sort of dreamy happiness, and Michael claimed a great deal of her time. John Daly was much occupied too, in examining his stock, and arranging everything in order, for it had been agreed that Michael Thorn should take charge of the farm, and live with them.

The parish church was about one mile distant from the farm; it was a rather low stone building covered with ivy; with a low door, and long narrow windows. Here Father Blake officiated and felt very happy to tie the knot for Michael and Eily, as he had known them from early childhood.

The morning rose in unclouded splendor —it was rather warm, but a sweet balmy atmosphere, and the lovely blue of the sky was unbroken, save by occasional floating, light fleecy clouds, that passed over the blue in graceful sweeps, and looked like lace work—and while looking, you might almost fancy them—some more decorations for the bride—some fairy scarfs, or veils.

Every face was bright—no clouds—no long faces—no tears—she was not going away—she was only going to church—to come back to them the wife of Michael Thorn, and the same little Eily at home—the sunshine of the house. There was a hushed brightness and happiness about Eily —she walked quietly, and spoke more softly—she smiled gently—instead of laughing merrily, as she was wont to do—a sort of subdued gladness hung over her—she seemed to feel the dignity of the proud title she was about to assume of wife— and the rank of matron; and the sense of the great duties and obligations belonging to them no doubt filled her mind, and engrossed her thoughts; but she only grew softer and sweeter— more gentle and loving.

Soon arrayed by Kathleen's hands in the pure

robe of simple white muslin—the tulle veil caught in the golden waves of her hair by a spray of orange blossoms—she made a sweet picture of perfect innocence and beauty, and descending she presented herself for inspection before departure for the church.

Winny declared she was her blessed wean, and showered every blessing on her head. Pat declared she was the "sweetest young lady, and the very beautifullest to be seen in the whole County Galway;" while Eily smiling gently as she passed from one to the other—crossed over to where her father stood in proud and stern admiration.

"Am I all right dear father?"

"Yes, dear child," exclaimed John Daly with fervor, as he clasped the little one in his arms. "You are, indeed, all that a fond parent could desire. May every blessing fall on your young head this day" Then taking her over to Michael Thorn, he added—"Here she is Michael— take good care of her—and may you see bright days." Eily placed her little hand confidingly on Michael's strong arm—one of Michael Thorn's brothers acted as best man. Kathleen and a young lady from Ballinasloe were the brides-maids. They all passed out in quiet happiness, and set out for the parish church. Father Blake was there to officiate, and the Nuptial Mass was said and the benediction given in a most impressive manner by the good old father. Eily with downcast eyes, and a soft blush mantling her cheek—walked slowly down the aisle, leaning on Michael's arm, and followed by the rest of the family—Winny and Pat bringing up the rear. The little Sunday-school children met her at the door with the sweetest flowers to scatter in her path. She stopped to greet many of them, for they were her scholars. The church was filled with old and young, and all gave their heart-felt blessing to the young and innocent one who had just received the sacrament of marriage. The last one who passed through the door of the little old-fashioned church was Father Blake—his white hair flowing down over his shoulders, and supporting himself with his strong oaken-stick. "I'll be with you," said he to the wedding party, and he jumped into the car to accompany them home. Having arrived there the neighbors gathered in, and they passed a pleasant evening—some merry music—a dance, and refreshments dispensed by Winny and Pat, wound up the day.

CHAPTER IX.

"*Art is long, and time is fleeting:
And our hearts tho' strong and brave,
Still like muffled dreams are beating
Funeral marches to the grave.*"

Years have passed quietly by. Eily is the gentle, pretty matron, surrounded by a troop of healthy, happy children. Michael has managed the farm, entirely to the satisfaction of John Daly, who has quietly settled down into Grandpa—whose special chair—seat at the table, and every wise, or pretty speech is duly venerated by the growing household. Winny is in her element among the young brood over whom she rules as a sort of household divinity—she dispenses her favors with great equity and justice—but does not allow that her *childher* ever do anything wrong, or commit any misdemeanor whatever, but that they are the most blessed weans that God ever bestowed on any parents.

Soon after Eily's marriage, Kathleen entered the convent at Ballinasloe, of the Sisters of Mercy —there she too was arrayed in her bridal dress— her beautiful hair was cut off, and the black habit, cap and veil robed her queenly form, and only seemed to make her look more beautiful still. She took the name of Sister Adele, and was known far and wide for her numerous acts of simple charity and mercy. She never wearied in doing good. The aged and infirm—little children —mothers—sons—fathers—all went to her for comfort of some kind—none appealed in vain, and all went away carrying with them, each their own particular consolation, and showering blessings on the sweet patient sister, who never turned a deaf ear to their many wants and miseries—and who worked with untiring zeal in her mission— with a true heart in her vocation. But Kathleen had inherited her mother's delicacy of constitution —seen perhaps in that unearthly purity of complexion. She gradually declined, and soon she appeared a ghost of her former self, and as she flitted about on her heavenly missions of love and charity—her slight form grew thinner and thinner until she looked in her spiritual beauty and brightness, as though she were truly a spirit from that land whose peopling is of angels. As she passed her people with her shadowy form, little children would clasp their hands—mothers would sigh—and the old would stop and say: "Soon she will vanish from our midst—there's a look of Heaven about her—something not of earth—she don't belong here, anyhow." Too soon, too true were these prophetic warnings. One day she was unable to go on the rounds of ministering grace and mercy. The cuckoo had scarcely sung his first spring note, when it was announced that Sister Adele would never visit them again. Great was the gloom among the neighboring poor. Mothers spoke in whispered accents long, with hands pressed upon their hearts. Little children stood in groups, with tears in their eyes, to talk of the dear Sister who had taught them all they knew, and shared every little sorrow and joy. Eily and her father had paid many visits to Ballinasloe lately, to see the sweet Sister who was pluming her wings for the last flight. Her lessons and advice to Eily were full of the beauty of holiness—and the sorrow of the father and daughter, though deep, was chastened and subdued. One morning they were sent for in haste —she had just breathed her last. They reached there only in time to see that lovely face calm in the repose of the last sleep of death. There she lay in all her heavenly beauty, which the dark habit only enhanced; the slender white fingers folded on her breast. It was not death, but the sweet sleep of an angel. You felt with all its force that line—" Tell me my soul, can this be death ?"—No—it was the sleep of the angels. The Mother Superior stood at the foot of the bed. Eily worn out with weeping knelt at the side. The stern old father stood erect with arms folded. On his face you read-"My God! I gave her to Thee long ago." Two or three curly-headed children opened the door and peeped in—then crept away in childish fear and dread of the solemn presence of *Death*. "Come in children," said the mother-"fear not! the room, I think, is filled with Angels." The children approached holding by one another, they drew nearer and kissed her robe, while tears flowed down their cheeks, and sobs broke forth. There she lay in calm majestic beauty—a sweet smile played about her mouth. Farewell! Kathleen. She had entered the " *Life Everlasting.*"

The Lame Foot.

Adrienne Durozel, as well as several of her little friends, attended the school of Miss Menais; but, although she was very intelligent, it was very rarely that she obtained a high place in class, because study fatigued her. She learned her lessons very poorly, and executed her tasks with negligence; and when she was not watched, she passed her time in reading fairy tales or plays instead of studying.

The evening before the day for the lesson in geography, Madame Durozel said to her daughter: "My child, you are going to draw to-day the map of Europe. I am obliged to go out, which annoys me extremely; you must, my dear one, give much application to this work, in order to have, to-morrow, the eye and hand sufficiently well practised, so that you will be able to draw this map well when you are in class: for you know that Miss Menais does not permit you to have any model. Promise me to work as if I were near you; for, if I believed that you would lose time in my absence, I would sooner neglect my business than leave you. I should be so happy to see you hold a high place in your class."

"Attend to your business, and be happy, dear Mamma: I will not leave my map until it is finished, and I will even correct it with the Atlas."

So Adrienne traced her degrees, and drew the outlines of some of the northern countries. Having need of a pair of compasses, she went to look for one in her father's study. There she saw upon the table four little volumes, entirely new. She took the first and opened it, to look at the title and the engravings: it was the "Swiss Family Robinson."

The child wished to read only the first chapter, but, allowing herself to be carried away by the interest of the story, she continued to read, notwithstanding the voice of her conscience, which reproached her for deceiving her Mother and breaking her word that she had given her. But the temptation was great, and she had not strength to resist it.

Adrienne must have read for an hour, more or less, when she heard her Mother enter; she quickly put back the book in the place from which she had taken it, and ran through the parlor, to return and place herself again at her work.

In passing before the clock, she glanced up, and saw with confusion that nearly three hours had passed since Madame Durozel had gone out.

Overwhelmed by the fault that she had not the courage to confess, on hearing her Mother approach, Adrienne threw herself full length upon the sofa. When Madame Durozel entered, she was frightened on seeing the distorted face of her little girl.

"Oh! Mercy! my child, what has happened to you?" cried the poor Mother: "are you ill?"

"Oh! yes, Mamma," stammered Adrienne with confusion; "I am suffering horribly with pain in my right foot and leg."

Madame Durozel, much alarmed, rang for Briggitta, the nurse, who took care of the child, and sent her for a physician.

When he arrived, they took off her shoes and stockings, whilst she uttered cries of anguish The Doctor examined the foot and leg, but could discover no trace of any injury. He seemed much astonished at such excessive pain without intermission. He ordered an application of belladonna leaves, dipped in laudanum, to be administired morning and evening.

They put the invalid to bed, and Briggitta established herself near her. Her father came to see her; and, to enable her to endure the illness with patience, he brought the four volumes of the "Swiss Family Robinson," that he had bought the evening before, to give her if she had attained a high place in composition. He little imagined that the little girl had already seen them.

This comedy lasted for five days, during which time Madame Durozel did all in her power to entertain her child, and gratify all her fancies; but weariness took possession of Adrienne. The weather was magnificent; she would have liked very much to have gone to the Tuileries, which is a number of large and beautiful gardens attached to the Palace of the Tuileries in Paris, and which is beautifully laid out in parterres of the richest flowers, and where children enjoy themselves very much on bright days; and Adrienne in spite of the terrible accident, was pining to be with her young companions in these lovely gardens where rich and poor, young and old enjoy themselves to their hearts content, and forgetting the part she was acting, she became very uneasy in her bed.

Briggitta, who observed her, and who was beginning to doubt the reality of the lameness of the foot, resolved to assure herself of the truth.

In the evening, at the regular hour, she prepared the dressing;—Adrienne was so much absorbed in reading the "Fairy of the Clouds," and the nurse dressed her foot so tenderly, that the invalid forgot to utter the accustomed groans.

Briggitta most adroitly placed the bella-donna poultice on the well foot.

The Doctor, who came every morning to see how this singular case was progressing, was stupefied with amazement when he saw the dressing placed on the other foot. He was going to exclaim, when he raised his eyes, and met Briggitta's glance. He arranged the flannel and bandages as usual, and touched the foot, which caused Adrienne to jump, and drew from her slight exclamations of pain.

"You suffer, then, all the time, my child?" said he.

"A little less than yesterday Doctor," replied the little one, with a perfectly composed air.

"And the other foot, how is that?"

"Oh! perfectly well: see!" and she performed various evolutions with her right foot.

"Come here quickly, Madame," cried the Doctor to Madame Durozel, who entered,— "come and see this wonder! Behold! for six days I have endeavored to cure your daughter's right foot, without succeeding, whilst Briggitta, by applying the dressing to the left-foot, has performed this miracle! But I very much fear that an evil still more grave will be the result of all this, and which will demand all your care."

And taking his hat, he went out, casting a cold glance on Adrienne, who perceived then, for the first time, the trick that her nurse had played.

She was so overcome with shame, when she saw that her deception was discovered, that she burst into tears.

"Oh! my child!" said Madame Durozel, more afflicted than her daughter, perhaps, "how could you descend to such a falsehood, and how could you persevere in it so long?" Has your conscience remained mute during the six days that you have passed in your bed?"

"No, in truth, dear Mamma," replied Adrienne, sobbing, "truly I was ashamed; but I did not know how to extricate myself from the position into which I had so stupidly placed myself."

And she related to her Mother how it had come to pass.

"My daughter, shall I then no longer be able to repose my trust in your integrity, nor belief in your word? Ah! you have caused me in this moment the keenest grief that I have ever felt; for *lying* is a thing so *base* and so degrading, that it always leaves upon the soul a *stain* most difficult to efface; and the idea alone that you know *how to lie*, fills me with grief."

"Dear, good Mother, punish me, for I have well merited it; but do not take away from me your confidence! nothing shall cost me too much to regain it, I assure you; put me to the proof, and you will see. Oh! above all, above all, do not grieve any more, my Mother, I beg and entreat."

From this day Adrienne studies with great dilgence, and the peace and happiness of the family, troubled for a time by this incident, are now entirely reestablished. But the poor child can never look in the face of the Doctor who attended her, and whose presence revives all her remorse.

Eulalie,

or

The Little Miser.

Eulalie possessed much intelligence and sensibility; but these bright qualities were tarnished by one great defect: she was a little miser. "A miser at ten years old? "I hear you say gentle readers, this is impossible"! This odious vice (one for which there is no excuse) did not render her happy. First she deprived herself of the *matchless* happiness of giving; then she gave herself up to a continual contest between her good heart, which led her to help the poor, and her love of money, which, alas! presented her always.

The nurse who had taken tender care of Eulalie when she was little, and from the time of her infancy, had married a carpenter in the neighborhood, and was dying of a decline: the little girl went to see her every day. The doctors, not being able to save her, permitted them to gratify all her whims and fancies: and the sick woman had many.

When Eulalie found at Home that which would please her nurse, she carried it to her eagerly; but when she wished for something that she was compelled to buy, the child never had the generosity to procure it for this woman, who had so tenderly nursed her, and whom she loved, nevertheless, so much.

One day,—it was toward the end of June,—Eulalie found the sick woman more disturbed than usual.

"What is the matter with you to-day, my dear nurse, "said she to her, "that you seem so uneasy?

"My darling, I dare not tell you; it is too silly." "Yes; tell me—do!"

"Ah! well, I have a foolish desire to taste a melon, and I cannot help crying because I cannot gratify this wish."

Has the Doctor forbidden it?"

"Oh! no, truly he has not."

"Why, then, can you not have some?"

"It is this: you know, my dear little one, melons are very rare at this season; it would cost too much for poor working people to buy them. Nevertheless, in vain have I told myself that; I cannot console myself for being deprived of tasting melons this year."

"Console yourself—they will not always be so dear."

"Yes; but then—where will I be?" and the poor woman wept in speaking thus. Her tears moved Eulalie: on returning Home she asked her mother if there were any melons in the house; and as the reply was in the negative, she went up-stairs to her room, and took from the bureau-drawer a very little box, of which she carried the key. She opened it, and regarded complacently the little treasure that it contained. Her heart beat quickly on touching all these small pieces of silver, she arranged them on the bureau, counted them, and was so completely absorbed and delighted with this work, that she forgot entirely for what purpose she had taken them from the box.

She finished at last by replacing them, and only *then* did she think of her nurse. Sighing, she took three beautiful pieces of one franc each; but at the moment, when about closing the box, she thought she would not take them, and the three pieces were sent back to join the others. The next day, she took from the table a plate of very highly flavored strawberries; she sugared them well, and then carried them to the sick woman.

"They are very beautiful, "said she, thanking the child; but as for me, poor darling, I wish for nothing but melon; I have dreamt of it all night in my fever. Must I die, then, without having had one taste?"

Struck with these words, Eulalie looked at her nurse more attentively, and was singularly struck with her changed appearance.

She wept.

"Do not grieve, my child, "said the poor woman: "it is much better to die than to be a burden upon your family If I had only one mouthfull of melon, to restore my appetite!" and she cast upon Eulalie a beseeching look which seemed to say much.

The little girl understood it, and returned Home, perfectly resolved, this time, to give a last satisfaction to the faithfull nurse who had taken such good care of her in her infancy. She open- again the little box, took out the three pieces of silver, put them in her pocket, and went down to attend to her daily duties. From time to time she put her hand in her pocket, to have the pleasure of feeling the three pieces; later still, she said to herself that she could very well postpone the purchase of the melon until the next day, and that *then* perhaps, the fancy of her nurse would have passed away.

The poor woman *expired in the night*! Eulalie was inconsolable for not having given her this *last pleasure,* for evidently she expected it from the child of whom she had taken so much care. The beseeching look of the sick woman followed her every where, and awakened salutary remorse in her conscience, which, I beleive, has corrected her of the most shameful avarice.

The Good Old Priest
and
The Snuff Box.

One beautiful spring morning the carriage of Madame Lemaire stopped before the steps of a little country house of the Bourbonnais, which rested in the midst of a lovely garden, like a nest of nightingales in a rose bush.

Little Sarah, a child of eight years of age, descends first; and they had not finished unloading the carriage, when she had already plundered the groves to gather a large bouquet for her mother; then escaping again, she ran to the Priest's house, to see the good old priest who had baptized her, and who was going to prepare her for her first communion. In short, she did not return until dinner time.

"Well, my child," said Madame Lemaire, "how is our good pastor?"

"Oh! mamma, he is very thin, and very pale."

"He is not at all well, the dear gentleman," said the gardener's wife, who was assisting Madame Lemaire, in arranging some flowers. "During the severe winter that has just passed, he has not been kept warm enough for a man of his age, and for more than six months he has only drank water."

"Oh! dear, dear! why is that?"

"It is this, you see, madame, the snow remained a long time on the ground this year; work was scarce in the cottages, and food also, for the potatoes were frozen. The heart of the good priest bled on seeing all of this misery; then he went to sleep in the little room, and sent away the bed from his large chamber, in which he placed a stove that was lit in the evening; every one came to warm themselves at their ease. As he knew very well that no one had enough to eat in the town, he contrived to have some good soup made, and everyone had their porringer full, morning and evening. Now all his wood is gone, and he has finished by selling his wine stand. Although he had made such a collection to give away, he was still filled with anxious fears that it was not enough to relieve the wants of the poor people. Then he has denied himself food, to give to others."

"Mamma" cried Sarah," I know now why I

have not seen his beautiful ivory crucifix in its usual place; and why he, who thought so much of his large silver snuff box, should now use one of birch bark instead."

He has sold everything, the good man, even his three spoons, and his large silver goblet; and he eats now with a wooden spoon, like all the poor people of his parish."

The good priest came in the evening, to pay a visit to Madame Lemaire.

She invited him to dine with her the next day, and placed her purse in his hands, begging him to distribute the contents as alms, because he knew so well how to dispense them—so much better than she did.

In the evening, when Sarah kissed her mother good night, she said, gazing at her with a most beseeching look:

"Ah! Mamma, if you would permit me—"

"Permit you to do what, my child?"

"Permit me to buy back the snuff box of my pastor! You know that papa gave me a little money, when he bade me good-bye."

"Yes, certainly, my child; I will permit you to buy back the snuff box of our good pastor! We will go to-morrow, without delay, to the city; I wish to recover the crucifix upon which he has been accustomed to cast his first glance when he awakened, and before which he said his first morning prayer. Embrace me, my dear one; I am most happy that we have had the same idea. We must set out very early to-morrow morning, in order to return in time for dinner, and you know that the route is long and tedious, so, do not sleep to long!"

Useless advice!—the child was awake before day; the hope of giving pleasure to the venerable priest, and the fear of not being able to find again the snuff box, agitated her so much.

Arriving in the city, Madame Lemaire easily found the silversmith who had bought the silverware from the charitable priest; the old snuff box was still at the shop, to Sarah's great joy; but he had sold the goblet and the spoons.

The person who had purchased the crucifix was induced to give it up to Madame Lemaire, only upon the condition that he should return for it some day, for it was a true masterpiece of art.

On returning home, Sarah and her mother found the good priest reading his breviary, and waiting for them. They told the maid to replace the crucifix in the alcove in the parsonage.

The old man who took snuff very frequently, had his snuff box almost always near him. At dinner, whilst very busy telling of a family who had just been ruined by fire, Sarah substituted, without his perceiving it, the *silver box* for that of the bark. The priest took it mechanically, whilst continuing to speak; but feeling the coldness of the metal, he stopped and looked at it; then he lifted it to his lips, while large tears flowed slowly down his cheeks.

"Will you," said he, "excuse the weakness of an old man?" *My mother* always used this box as long as she lived."

Then seeing the radiant face of the little girl, who had fixed her tearful eyes upon him.

"My daughter," said he to her, "God will bless thee; for *the purest incense that one can offer Him, is the happiness that we give to our neighbor.*

Lies in Action and By Omission.

Sister Anne Joseph was a holy woman, who kept a charity school in her small town. She loved the children who came to her class, as if she had been their own mother; she also desired to correct their faults, and that she often found very difficult. The poor sister, had above all, much trouble in making them understand how displeasing lying was to Almighty God, and how much evil it produced in the world.

"Sister," one of the best scholars said to her one day, "I assure you that we never tell a falsehood."

You believe so, my child, because you say nothing that is not true; but it is not alone by speech that we may deceive. You may *act a lie*; and, by omitting to speak the truth when it might benefit your neighbor, you may *lie by omission*.

The children did not understand her.

Some days after, Sister Anne Joseph observed a little girl, the very one who had said that *she* never told a lie, wiping her mouth very frequently. On observing her very closely, the sister perceived that, every time that she pretended to wipe her mouth, she slyly slipped in a cherry, notwithstanding that it was forbidden to eat in class.

She called to her from her desk. "Marinette, you are lying at this moment!" "I, Sister!" replied the child, whose speech was slightly affected by the cherry that she had in her mouth—"But I said nothing!" "That is very true, you have not spoken; but you have been eating cherries by stealth, all the while pretending to wipe your mouth. Ah! well, my daughter, *this is a lie in action.*"

Marinette blushed, and a smothered laugh passed through the benches.

A little later, in unfolding her work, little Sophie lost her needle. The Sister had seen it. However, the child continued to move her arm, and one would think that she was sewing with zeal.

"Sophie," said the Sister, "bring me your work."

The little girl obeyed with a marked dislike.

But what have you done to-day, my child? "Your work is just as it was yesterday."

It was necessary to confess that she had lost her needle.

"Ah! well, Sophie, when you have the appearance of working with so much zeal, and, nevertheless, do nothing, is not that a lie, although you do not say a word?"

Sophie returned, much confused, to her place, with a new needle, and the smothered laugh commenced again.

Among those who smiled was a large, fair complexion girl, who seemed to study her lessons with great attention; but, as her neighbors were making great efforts to keep from laughing, Sister Anne Joseph, whom they could not deceive very easily, suspected the studiousness of the blonde, and, passing softly behind her, took her book, and saw that she held it upside down. Again one more who *lied in action!*

"My dear little ones," said she, "you laugh at the faults of your companions, and you forget too easily that you, too, commit faults. Such conduct is wrong. Do you not know, my children, that you must be good, above all? Without goodness all the rest is nothing."

The Sister had remarked that, for some time, one of her scholars, who was very mild, and very industrious, never arrived in time for the opening of the morning class. She reproached her; and the child, who was very timid, wept, without giving the least excuse. Sister Anne Joseph, very much astonished to find that all her remonstrances were perfectly useless, made some inquiry in the part of the town where the little Marie Louis lived. She learned that this child, who had no mother, and who kept house for her father as well as she could, did still more. She went every morning to wash the linen for a sick neighbor, and all this, poor as she was herself. Her companions knew this well!

After class, in the evening, the Sister said to them:

"You heard me every day reproaching Marie Louise for her want of punctuality. The poor child never excused herself, and I continued to blame her negligence. I hear that this good little one renders a service every day to a sick neighbor. You all knew it, and not one came to tell me; and you have let me scold your companion, when you knew well that she did not merit it. See, my little friends, that is what I call *a lie by omission*; because you have omitted to speak the truth when you would have done much good by making it known. Recollect well, my children, that you never must be silent when, by speaking, you may be useful or agreeable to your neighbor; for God has said: "*Thou shalt love thy neighbor as thyself.*"

Vanity.

There lived in Paris a young married lady, by the name of Madame Julia Bercy. This lady was very beautiful and very intelligent, but extremely frivolous, and was entirely occupied with the follies of the world. She was what they call in France *une mondaine*, which means a very worldly person. She passed her time in making visits, and in entertainments of all kinds, completely occupied with displaying her elegant dresses and beautiful jewels. Every morning she passed an endles time in arranging her hair, polishing her nails, and perfuming her whole person. She took particular care of her hands, which were very beautiful; and in order to preserve their whiteness better, she wore gloves even at night, while sleeping.

She did not pass any time even with her children, but gave them up entirely to the care of their nurse; scarcely did their mother kiss them, even once a day.

Although Madame Bercy was very rich, she never had any money to give as alms, nor time to think of the poor; for she spent every thing to satisfy her vanity; she did not even find time to render a service to any one.

She had an uncle, who was an excellent clergyman; he frequently spoke to her on this subject, using the most forcible and eloquent language, in order to touch her heart which, alas! vanity had so hardened.

But, although she always listened to him with great deference, she never became any more reasonable or sensible, because her vanity was still a great deal stronger than the affection that she felt for her uncle.

One morning he called on her to make a new attack. He found her seated before a large mirror; she was arranging her hair in different styles, trying on head-dresses, and regarding herself in the most smiling and admiring manner.

The worthy priest was struck, for the first time, with the beauty and extreme whiteness of the hands of his niece; and inspired with a thought from heaven, he said to her:

"Julia, I have decided to fatigue you no longer with my useless sermons; I will be silent then, henceforth. However, I keep silence upon one condition, which will be very easy for you to fulfil: it is, that every morning you say three words only."

"My dear uncle, I am entirely disposed to satisfy you."

"But Julia, you must promise me solemnly not to fail to do so."

"I promise you solemnly, my dear Uncle."

"It is only necessary to see your hands, to understand that you have taken great care of them."

"I do take great care of them, indeed," replied Julia, looking at her hands with complacency; every morning I rub them with almond paste, and then I perfume them with myrtle water or vervain."

"Ah! well, every morning, after having rubbed and perfumed your hands, you must say, on looking at them and turning them three times: "Hands, you will decay! Hands, you will decay! Hands, you will decay!

"Be assured I will not fail to do so; but let me tell you that I think it is a very singular idea!"

"As you wish, my dear niece; old men oftentimes have their eccentricities, which you must regard with compassionate charity. Adieu! I shall rest easy since you have given your word."

The next day, in the morning Madame Bercy, on making her toilet, did not fail to turn her beautiful hands three times, after having carefully washed and perfumed them, and repeated the words that her uncle had dictated. She did it for several days in succession, without attaching much importance to it.

One morning, however, she listened while pronouncing three times, "Hands, you will decay!"

"My uncle was right," thought she, "in saying that old men often have strange ideas!"

The following day, after having said the three words, she looked at her hands with a kind of compassion, saying: "It would be a great pity, truly, that they should decay, they are so beautiful!"

Each day led to some new reflection. "Indeed they will decay, nevertheless," cried she in a loud voice. "Those who praise them to-day would look on them with horror if they should see them then."

Another time she reflected: "But, if my hands decay, my body also will decay! Of what use will my beautiful ornaments be then, which now are my glory and my happiness?

On this day she closed her doors to visitors, so that her meditations might not be disturbed. The next day she asked herself: "When the moment arrives for me to leave this world, what shall I be able to say I have done? And passing over her entire life in her memory, she could not recollect a single good action, not the slightest duty fulfilled: nothing, in short, that she could lay at the feet of our Lord, in order to disarm His just severity, and this thought frightened her.

In order to escape from the sadness that overwhelmed her in spite of herself, she made the most beautiful toilet, to go to a brilliant entertainment that was given the same evening. On casting a last glance at her mirror, she found herself less beautiful than usual: looking down upon her arms adorned with bracelets, and upon her hands loaded with rings, she experienced an indefinable uneasiness, and she hastened to put on her gloves.

When Madame Bercy entered the ball-room a murmur of admiration arose from every corner of the drawing-room, and she experienced one moment of lively pleasure, in observing that, in the midst of these new and elegant toilets, her own was the freshest and the most brilliant.

But after having looked around, and examined every one, she commenced thinking that these gay men and these silly women, devoted to pleasure, would soon become nothing more than dust, and that all of them, like her hands, would one day decay.

"What reply will they make to our Lord," said she to herself, "when he demands of them an account of the soul that he gave them?"

Then she thought of her mother, so pious, and so good to every one. Then the beauty of all this sparkling youth disappeared before her eyes; she saw herself such as she would be at the day of judgment, and her heart was troubled.

Not finding any pleasure in this entertainment, she left it. On returning home, she went into the nursery, which she very rarely visited. The children slept sweetly and softly together, and they appeared to her so beautiful, that she believed that she had never seen them until this moment. She did not know how she had been able to abandon these dear little ones to the care of strangers.

In thinking of these two little angels, tucked in so warmly under their elder-down coverlet, she thought how many little children had no covering for their beds, no fire to warm them, no bread to satisfy their hunger—and she wept.

The next day Madame Bercy rose much earlier than usual; she sought the nursery and her children, for she wished to dress them herself. Her uncle, who had not been to see her since the promise that she had made, came in this morning to see her, by chance. He found her combing the fair hair of her little girl. The good priest, going toward her with his heart full of holy joy, took her beautiful hand, which he kissed with tenderness.

"Oh my Uncle!" cried Madame Bercy, "finish your work, and sustain me in my good resolutions by your pious counsels! Guided by you, these hands, which will one day decay, shall henceforth sow benefits. I wish to fulfil all my duties now, in order that God may not reject my soul when it will have left this perishable body, that I have idolized for so long a time.

Madame Bercy persevered, and became the most devoted mother of her family, whom the poor and unfortunate blessed every day. When she compared the actual and present happiness that she was deriving from the faithful discharge of all her duties, with that which she used to receive from the vain ornaments and frivolous amusements in old times, and which she now had renounced, she said to the good priest, with the most heartfelt gratitude: "Ah! my dear uncle! what would I have become if you had not imposed upon me the obligation of saying every morning: "Hands, you shall decay! Hands, you shall decay! Hands, you shall decay!

Gratitude and Integrity.

A Tale Founded on Fact.

In the southern part of Auvergne, a short distance from Clermont, lived an honest farmer who, by divers accidents, was entirely ruined, notwithstanding his great goodness. He was a widower, and not having married until he was fifty-two years of age, he was already an old man when his only son had reached the age of ten years.

This good peasant, named Furcy, lived in a little dilapidated cabin; he worked all day, and his modest salary scarcely sufficed for his subsistence and that of little Bourgingnon, his only child; however, he kept a goat, destined only for the nourishment of Bourgingnon. The poor father deprived himself of every thing, in order to provide for the wants of his son; but at last his misery became such, that he was obliged to send him to Paris to seek his fortune: a wagoner, one of his friends, agreed to take him there gratis. This wagoner did his best to console the unfortunate Furcy.

"Your little Bourgingnon," said he to him, is prudent and intelligent; besides, he is robust; accustomed to climb our mountains, he will be able to do the errands better than another; and then I will establish him in the street St. Honoré, next to the new house of the Bernardines. I have there some acquaintances, amongst them that of the porter Chassin, who is young, and a very good man: I tell you that he will make friends with Bourgingnon, and that he will be very useful to him."

These promises softened a little the grief of Furcy; he gave the most tender blessings to his son. Bourgingnon, in tears, promised him to return at the end of six months. During the journey, which was a very happy one, he often wept; the wagoner sang. Notwithstanding his grief, Bourgingnon did not lose an occasion of making himself useful. Perched upon the large cart, he hastened to get down at the least accident; he astonished the wagoner by his strength, his address, and his agility; and he finished by gaining his affection completely.

At last, on arriving at Paris, Bourgingnon was much surprised to find that this city was much larger than Clermont. The wagoner, according to promise, presented him, the same day, to the porter Chassin; he received him well, and bestowed upon him the most unequivocal marks of benevolence and interest. He obtained permission for him to pass his nights under a cart-shed which was in the court-yard; besides, he gave him something to eat; and after the next day, he spoke in his favor to some of the lodgers, and inspired them with the desire to see his *protegé*. Every one was charmed with the sprightliness and the refinement of the little one from Auvergne; they promised to engage him as errand boy, when he was a little better acquainted with the streets of Paris. Bourgingnon acquired this knowledge quickly, thanks to the advice and information of his patron, Chassin, and then he had much practice.

Notwithstanding his provincial Jargon, he made himself understood perfectly; he was so diligent, so exact, and so faithful, that they preferred him to the most experienced errand porters, and they always paid him with an especial liberality.

Whilst Bourgingnon prospered in Paris, his poor father in Auvergne, endured the most painful fatigues of labor, the agonies of misery, and the torments of paternal uneasiness. He was not relieved in expense by the departure of his child; for not only did he not wish to profit by the particular efforts of Bourgingnon, but he had formed the project of putting aside for him some little savings of his own work. "I shall have at least, when dying," he said, "the consolation of leaving him a good little sum for an inheritance."

This idea gave great courage to Furcy, notwithstanding the exhaustion of his physical strength. One morning, in the month of December, he was returning on foot slowly toward home, when, yielding to his lassitude, he was obliged to stop and seat himself on a stone. He found that he was at the foot of the famous mountain whose summit was inhabited by the respectable family of Pinon.* "Alas!" said Furcy raising his eyes toward the mountain. "If I could reach there, I should find all the assistance of which I have need, but it will be necessary, perhaps, for me to

---

* A community celebrated for rich and virtuous farmers, who were the possessors of the mountain and all the surrounding fields, forming a sort of little republic, having their own particular laws, and of whom the father or the grandfather of the family was the chief. Their dress, their piety, their simple manner, seemed to reproduce and realize all the traditions of the Golden Age. It is not known if it were through a happy forgetfulness that the Revolution left them to live on the crest of this mountain, in order, peace, and a happy security, so much greater, because it was founded on religion and filial piety.—

die here, so near the best friends of the poor traveller: they are there, they cannot hear me, and I cannot profit by their compassion and their charity."

However, the unfortunate Furcy, making an effort, and leaning strongly on his stick, tried to take some steps upon the steep road to the mountain; but he could not continue, and, without his stick, he would have had a dangerous fall; then, losing all hope, he thought of his child, and he could not restrain his tears; but calling to his aid Him who always hears us, he invoked God, and asked Him to bless his son; then resigning himself to his fate, and trusting in Divine Providence, he crossed his arms on his breast, and closing his eyes, fainted!

A few moments after, a young Pinon, returning to the mountain in his pleasure car, perceived the old man; he approached, and seeing that he had lost consciousness, he took him on his car, and continued his way. During the trip Furcy recovered his senses. The sight of a human face caused him such joy, that he was restored at once; and when he looked at the young man, whose mild physiognomy expressed so much tender compassion, he believed that he saw a liberating angel.

Arrived at the dwelling of the Pinon's, they made him enter the large and beautiful kitchen which served as a dining-room and parlor for all the family. The old man remarked, on entering, fifteen or sixteen young girls, clothed uniformly in brown stuff, and wearing on their heads long white veils; this modest ornament distinguishing them from the married women.

Each one held in her hand a distaff and spun. Their mothers and grandmothers, seated opposite to them, spun also, but with the wheel. This interesting reunion, which offered the contrast of grave experience, perhaps a little severe, with such sweet and timid innocence, charmed the eyes of the old man. The young girls rose at his approach, and seated him in the chimney corner, in the large *"arm-chair of hospitality,"* this was the name that they gave in this house to the easy and well-stuffed chair that was appropriated for the sick or weary traveller. When there was no stranger in the room, the arm-chair remained empty. Two young girls hastened to build up the fire, to warm the old man.

There was always in this house a separate room for an infirm clergyman or octogenarian uncle or great-uncle of the masters of this immense farm; for from time immemorial, in each generation, some young member of the family entered the seminary, and became a priest; and, if it happened that he was no longer in a condition to exercise the functions of the holy ministry, he was received with veneration into this peaceful asylum. At this epoch there was one there of eighty-six years of age. As Furcy found himself much better in the afternoon, he expressed a desire to receive the blessing of the pious and venerable clergyman. They led him to him: he was in his oratory. Furcy experienced a joy, mingled with hope, on seeing an old man who was twenty-four years older than himself; and his soul was filled with sweet consolation when he heard his holy exhortations, and received from his hands a blessed rosary. On his return to the hall, Furcy found there the young girls who sang hymns together, for it was the eve of a great feast. These sweet, fresh voices, so correct and so melodious, caused him such delight, that the following night, all through a tranquil sleep, he believed that he heard a heavenly concert of angels.

It was understood that Furcy should pass several days on the mountain. In the morning of the next day he went very early to say his prayers in the oratory, and after breakfast, as it was very fine weather, they led him into the orchard, where he took quite a long walk. The chief of the family led Furcy back to the house, and seated him in the *"arm-chair of hospitality."* At this moment they came to announce the visit of the Marchioness of—who was travelling with some other persons, and who did not wish to leave Auvergne without having visited the celebrated community of the Pinon. On entering the hall, the marchioness approached the fire, to warm herself, when the master of the house, turning toward her, said, showing her Furcy: "Madame, I cannot offer you the place of honor: you see it is occupied by a sick stranger."

As dinner was served, they invited the marchioness, who accepted with pleasure, as well as the friends whom she had brought with her. They placed themselves at the table with the good peasants: the marchioness admired their natural politeness. They spoke of the wonders of Auvergne, of those extinguished volcanoes which formed deep cavities or tunnels, where one could descend, and at the bottom of which one sometimes found some large chestnut trees. They boasted of the beauty of the grotto of Royat, with its numberless cascades, near Clermont. They did not forget to mention the fountains of pitch and those which had the quality of quickly petrifying the vegetable or animal substances that were plunged in it, receiving from them a sediment which acquired, with time, an excessive hardness. One of the young Pinons made a long eulogy on the extensive woodland, and the beauty of the castle on the estate of Randan.

Immediately after dinner the marchioness left her hosts, taking away with her from this mountain and these inhabitants a remembrance that time could never efface; and a few days after, Furcy, overcome with their kindness, and well rested from his fatigue, took once more the road to his little cabin.

While the good old man was employing all his failing strength to increase the sum that he intended for his child, the latter, on his part, was always thinking of his father, and working with an indefatigable zeal. He continued to be the protegé of those who lived in the new house of the Bernardines, and the honest porter Chassin felt a true friendship for him: he fed him almost entirely; for all the errands of the house he was generously paid. The proprietor, M. de Villiers, gave him, besides, what clothed him, and, in the course of time, coats, vests, and stockings; and he reserved for him a little room, very warm and very clean, in his house, so that Bourgingnon, lodged, clothed and fed, could, without wanting anything, put aside all the money that he earned. At the end of seven months he found himself the possessor of a little more than three hundred francs, so he made all the little preparations for his journey, and set out with joy to see and enrich his father, whom he found in pretty good health, but as poor as ever. He gave him his three hundred francs, which Furcy took immediately, and deposited secretly in a bag containing his old savings, which he had concealed in his straw bed.

In the last days of Autumn, Bourgingnon set out again to return to Paris. He found there the same asylum, the same patrons, and he never deviated from his good career: his conduct was always as pure, his life as active, as formerly.

Oue day, one of his patrons came to give him a letter to take to the Mission of Strangers, to the Abbé de Fenelon, the worthy clergyman who had established the old institution of the Savoyards, to which he joined the children from Auvergne and Limonsin. Bourgingnon gave the letter to the servant of the Abbé de Fenelon, and took it immediately to his master. At the end of a few minutes the servant returned to say to the little boy from Auvergne that the Abbé wished to speak to him; and he led him to the library. The Abbé received Bourgingnon with his natural kindness; he explained to him in a few words, the end of the association of the little Savoyards, and of the children of Auvergne and of Limonsin. "I know," added he, "that you are good and industrious; I will admit you with pleasure into this interesting society: this will be adopting you among the number of my children."

Bourgingnon, transported with joy, expressed his gratitude with the delicacy and ingenuousness of his age. He was at the height of his joy. At the moment when he was leaving, the good Abbé detained him, to attach to his buttonhole the honorable copper medal: it was understood that he would go every Sunday to receive christian instruction, which would give a firm foundation to his moral qualities.

Bourgingnon returned quickly to the Hotel des Bernardines, to thank his protectors, who had so well recommended him to the Abbé de Fenelon. He passed then, four or five months in Paris, at the end of which time, the possessor of one hundred crowns, he went to rejoin his father. But this reunion was very sad: the poor Furcy was in the most deplorable state of health; however, he received with a satisfied air the three hundred francs that his son gave him.

"My child," said he to him, "you will find this after me, for I feel that I have but a short time to live."

"Oh my father!" cried Bourgingnon, "we must pay attention to your health, and employ all this sum to establish it: I shall earn more."

The old man bowed his head, and did not reply; but he locked and concealed the money, promising inwardly not to spend a cent of it.

Bourgingnon wished, in vain, to call in a physician; Furcy always repeated that it was useless. Notwithstanding all the most tender cares, the old man declined sensibly. Feeling it himself, he one morning called his son, and, drawing from his mattress a linen bag that he had concealed there: "Take it, dear child," said he to him, "here are one thousand francs that I have laid up for you; you have gained by your labor the greater part of this sum, which belongs entirely to you. Although you are only in your thirteenth year, you will make, I am sure, a good use of this money: it may be the beginning of your fortune. Receive it with the most tender blessings of your father."

"Yes," said Bourgingnon sobbing, "I will make a good use of it."

After uttering these words, he threw himself on his kneess; his father blessed him, implored for him the divine protection, and recommended him to lock up his money in an old dilapidated bureau, but which had a lock and key on one of the drawers. Then falling back on his straw bed, the good old man ordered his son to go immediately for a priest. Bourgingnon, distracted, ran to the priest's house; from there he sent a messenger to Clermont to bring back a physician. He gave his courier six francs in advance, charging him to fly. Furcy received the sacraments, while his son, prostrated at the foot of his bed, prayed with a touching fervor. After having fulfilled his religious duties with an edifying piety, the old man had still time to embrace his son, and to press him to his heart. A few minutes after, he was struck with paralysis, and lost, at the same time, his consciousness and speech. The desolation of Bourgingnon was at its height; however, as his father still breathed, he still had some hope. He implored the priest, who was ready to leave the cabin, to send him the best nurse in the villiage, showing him the thousand francs, all his fortune, which he had decided to sacrifice to contribute to the recovery of his father. The priest touched with his filial piety, exhorted him to persevere, and assured him that God would reward it. The physician found Furcy in very great danger, "we may, perhaps, be able to relieve him," he said; "but it will be necessary to prescribe a treatment which will cost a great deal."

"Spare nothing," said Bourgingnon to the doctor, "dispose of all that I possess."

In short, Bourgingnon rented a bathing place, and sent to Clermont for all the medical prescriptions. He spent with liberality seven or eight louis, and as one nurse was not enough, he sent for a second.

Furcy remained for three months in the same condition; his son spared nothing to relieve him: it was necessary to buy sheets, towels, shirts. But all was in vain; the poor invalid, at last falling into the agonies of death, expired in the arms of his son, who spent nearly all that he had left to bury him.

These duties fulfilled, and all the expenses paid, there were only left for Bourgingnon about one hundred francs; but he consoled himself, saying, "at least the money has prolonged his existance a little."

He decided to leave Auvergne forever, and without any more delay he set out for Paris. He worked there at first without ambition, and with indolence; but the encouragement that his protectors gave him, restored his energy and his emulation.

The priest of his villiage had a relative in Paris, to whom he sometimes wrote. In one of his letters he related to him a part of what Bourgingnon had done for his father. This relation was acquainted with M. de Villiers, the proprietor of the Hotel des Bernardines. The recital touched M. de Villiers still more, as Bourgingnon had not boasted of his conduct, and he was contented with saying that he had had the misfortune to lose his father. They wished not to reward his filial piety, but to return him a little of his money: they made a little collection for him in secret, which amounted to three hundred and sixty francs, which they gave him without explaining the true motive of their liberality, for fear of renewing his grief. They were satisfied with exhorting him to work with activity, in order to show his gratitude to his patrons.

As Bourgingnon grew older, the Porter Chassin became more and more useful to him: two or three very rich persons came successively to lodge in this hotel; Chassin recommended to them, in a particular manner, his young friend, for whom he obtained from them a particular service, which was worth much money to Bourgingnon. As he knew how to read, and even write, very well, he rendered himself useful in a thousand ways; and at sixteen or seventeen years, having more than doubled his funds, he found himself the possessor of the sum of fifteen hundred francs. He pursued his career with the same success and the same good luck, without losing a single patron, and always encouraged by the good Chassin with a paternal zeal. He succeeded thus, at the age of thirty-eight years, in accumulating a sum of four thousand francs, which would have been still more considerable, if christian charity had not accustomed him, from his earliest youth, to distribute regular alms among the poor, and to give, from time to time, help to his unfortunate countrymen.

Heaven wishing, without doubt, to reward an industrious life, entirely consecrated to work and to virtue, called him in the most unexpected manner. One day, in one of his rounds, he fell and received a violent blow on the head; he paid but little attention to this accident, taking no precautions. An abcess formed on his head; soon his injuries began to show themselves: at last, at the end of forty days, he was so ill, that they were obliged to take him to the charity hospital.

There they declared that there was no hope of saving him; then, after having fulfilled all his religious duties, he sent for a notary, and dictated to him a will, in which, declaring that he had neither brother, nor sister, nor near relation, that he knew of, he disposed of the sum of four thousand francs in the following manner; five hundred francs to the charity hospital; four hundred francs for the poor; and one thousand crowns for his benefactor and his friend, Chassin, porter of the Hotel des Bernardines.

A few hours after having made and signed his will, he received a visit from Chassin, who had no suspicion of this legacy, and who, since his sickness, had come to see him regularly every day. Chassin was frightened at seeing him so weak:

judge of his grief on learning that it was a hopeless case. At last Bourgingnon, surrounded by all the consolations of religion and friendship, and strengthened by the most virtuous memories, expired sweetly on the evening of that day. Judge of the surprise of Chassin when they brought him the will of his friend, and the thousand crowns that he had bequeathed to him. After reflecting a short time, " No," said he, " I will not keep this money: my friend was only twelve years old when he left Auvergne; it is very possible that he had in that country, without knowing it, some poor relation, and it is of that that I wish to inform myself." Completely occupied with this idea, Chassin wrote immediately to Auvergne, to procure the most detailed information upon the subject. These searches were not unfruitful; they discovered, at the end of a few months, that there existed, near Thiers, a relation, though very far removed, of Bourgingnon, but who called himself Furcy, and who, the father of seven children, was in the most abject poverty. The virtuous Chassin did not hesitate, he sent immediately the thousand crowns to this man. He did not boast of this action; but, as he had employed many persons in the searches that he had made in Auvergne, this generous proceeding was generally known in the house. The master

of Chassin, M. de Villiers, was deeply touched by
it; and as he showed his admiration to Chassin,
the latter replied that he should have no merit for
what he had done; that this money would have
tormented him; and besides, he had no need of
such a sum, with so good a master, who would not
let him want for anything, and who surely would
take care of him in his old days.

M. de Villiers related this history to many persons, among others to M. Marmontel, who lodged in his hotel.

They had just instituted, a short time before, at
the French academy, a prize as a reward for the
most virtuous deed done in the course of the year.
This prize consisted of a gold medal, worth twelve
hundred francs. M. Marmontel finding, with
reason, that Chassin was worthy of it, proposed to
the academy to award it to him, and obtained it
for him.

Chassin was very much astonished when he
saw one morning some deputies from the French
academy entering his lodging. Among whom
was M. Marmontel; they announced to him that
they had brought him, in the name of the
academy, the gold medal, as a homage rendered
to his virtue. Chassin, understanding nothing of
this homage, asked an explanation of it; then,
more and more surprised, "Gentleman" said he,

"I am much obliged to you, but indeed I do not merit such a reward, for I only acted for my own repose."

The sublime simplicity of this reply fully proved how much Chassin was worthy of the honor that they awarded him.

This adventure made a great noise; every one wished to see Chassin, and even great ladies from the court went to pay him a visit. They took his portrait, which they placed in one of the halls of the French academy.

Providence truly rewarded Chassin. This human glory did not intoxicate him: he found the prize of his virtue in the affection of his excellent master, M. de Villiers. At the age of more than sixty years, Chassin became blind. M. de Villiers placed him upon one of his estates, and gave him a servant. There Chassin lived until he was eighty-four years of age—a constant object of the most tender care, always beloved and honored,—and his old age, until the end of his long life, was perfectly happy.

The Faithful Servant.

When James II, King of England, was compelled to abandon his kingdom, he took refuge in France, and Louis XIV gave him an asylum at St. Germain, where some of his faithful subjects, who had followed him, established themselves. Madame de Varonne, whose history I am going to relate to you, was of an Irish family, who had followed James II into Exile. While her husband lived, she enjoyed competency, and lived in easy circumstances; but having become a widow, and finding herself without protection, without relation, she could not obtain from court even a portion of the pension which was her husband's income. However, she wrote to the minister, and she sent several petitions. They replied to her that they would place her demand before the eyes of the King. Two years passed, without the slightest prospect of her hopes being realized.

THE FAITHFUL SERVANT. 109

At last, having renewed her solicitation, she received a formal refusal; it was no longer possible for her to remain blind to her fate. Her situation was deplorable; for two years she had been obliged, in order to live, to sell, successively, her silver and her furniture, piece by piece; there remained now no other resource. Her taste for solitude, her solid piety, and her bad health, had always held her aloof from society, and particularly so since the death of her husband. She found herself, then, without protection, without friends, without hope, denuded of every thing, plunged into frightful misery, and, to crown all her misfortunes, she was fifty years of age, and her health shattered. In this extremity she had recourse to the true Dispenser of consolations and of graces, to Him who could change her fate, or give her fortitude to enable her to support the severity of it with patience. She knelt and prayed to God with confidence; on rising, she was no longer disheartened; she felt a sweet calm spring up in her soul, and she looked with firm eyes on all that was terrible in her condition.

"Ah! well," said she, "since we must one day lose this frail existence, what does it matter, whether we be crushed by the last condition of misery, or by sickness? What does it signify whether we die under a canopy, or upon straw? Will my death be more painful, because I have nothing left to regret upon earth? No, without doubt; on the contrary, I shall need neither exhortation nor fortitude; I shall have no sacrifice to make. Abandoned by every one, I shall only think of Him who rules the universe; I shall see Him near, to receive me, to reward me, and I shall wait for death, as the most precious of his benefits."

"What fortitude!" you will say, my dear children: "Is it impossible to die without regretting life a little?" But remember that Madame de Varonne had no children; that she had no longer father or husband, and that there was no affection left for her in this world. Besides, religion can give this sublime resignation, and I have already told you that Madame de Varonne had a solid piety.

As she was reflecting on her sad destiny Ambrose, her servant, entered.

I must make you acquainted with this Ambrose. He was a man of forty years of age, who for twenty years, had served Madame de Varonne. Not knowing how to read or write, abrupt, silent, a grumbler, he had always the air of despising and looking down on his fellow-servants, and of sulking with his masters; his countenance wore a continual scowl, and his disagreeable temper rendered his services not very pleasant. However, his exact punctuality in the performance of all his duties, and his good conduct generally, had always caused him to be regarded as an excellent being, and a very valuable servant. They recognized in him only the essential qualities, and, besides, he possessed some sublime virtues; under an exterior, almost forbidding, he concealed the most tender and elevated soul.

Madame de Varonne, some time after the death of her husband, had sent away the people attached to her service, and retained only a cook, a maid, and Ambrose. At last she found herself compelled to discharge again these three servants. Ambrose, as I told you, entered. It was winter: he brought in a log of wood, and was going to put it on the fire, when Madame de Varonne said to him:

"Ambrose, I wish to speak to you."

The tone of emotion with which Madame de Varonne pronounced these words, struck Ambrose. Resting his log of wood on the floor, and looking at his mistress: "My God! Madame," said he, "what has happened?"

"Ambrose, do you know how much I owe the Cook?"

"You owe him nothing, Madame, nor myself, nor Mary; you paid us last month."

"Ah! so much the better: I did not remember

it. Ah! well, Ambrose, I charge you to tell the cook and Mary that I no longer have need of their services. And yourself, my dear Ambrose it is necessary that you should look for another situation."

"Another situation! what do you mean? I wish to die in your service; I wish never to leave you, no matter what happens."

"Ambrose, you do not know my position."

"Madame, you are not acquainted with Ambrose. Ah! well, if they have withdrawn your pension, and you have not the means of paying your people, send away the others immediately; but for myself, I have not merited to be chased away with them. I have not a mercenary soul, Madame."

"But, Ambrose, I am ruined, entirely ruined; All that I possess I have sold, and they have taken away my pension."

"They have taken away your pension? That cannot be."

"Nothing is more true, however, ah, good God! we must respect and adore the decrees of Providence, and submit to them without murmuring, my good Ambrose. However, in my misfortune, I experience a great consolation: it is that of feeling perfectly resigned, while so many beings upon earth, so many virtuous families, find themselves in the same situation in which I am placed.

I, at least, have no children: I alone will suffer. It is little to suffer."

"No, no," cried Ambrose, in a stifled voice, "no, you shall not suffer. I have hands, I know how to work."

"My dear Ambrose," interrupted Madame de Varonne, much moved, "I have never doubted your attachment; I will not abuse it now. This is all that I am waiting for: it is that you should go and rent for me a little room on the fifth story. I have still some money left; enough to suffice for two or three months. I will work, I will sew. Seek for me in St. Germain some customers. This is all that I ask of you, and all that you will be able to do for me."

Ambrose had remained immovable before his mistress, regarding her in silence; when she had finished speaking, he fell at her feet.

"Ah! my good mistress," cried he, receive the vow of poor Ambrose: "I engage to serve you until the end of my life, and with a better heart, with more respect and obedience, than I have ever done. For twenty years I have been nourished, clothed, by you; you have provided for me, you have made my life happy. I have very often abused your kindness and your patience. Ah! madame, pardon all the faults that I have committed toward you with my bad disposition.

I will repair them, be sure of it; I only ask length of days from the good God to accomplish it."

In finishing these words, Ambrose, in tears, rose and went out hastily, without waiting for a reply.

You may judge easily with what lively and deep gratitude the heart of Madame de Varonne was filled. At the end of a few minutes Ambrose returned; he held in his hand a little bag of skin. Laying it upon the Mantel, he said:

"Thanks to God, thanks to you, Madame, and to your good deceased husband, there are there, in that purse, thirty louis. This money came from you, and it belongs to you."

"Ambrose! The fruit of your savings for twenty years! I cannot accept it."

"When you had money, you gave it to me, when you have it no longer, I return it to you; money is only good for that. I know well that this little sum cannot extricate Madame from her embarrassment; but this is what I calculate to do. It must be that madame remembers that I am the son of a coppersmith, and that I have not forgotten my first trade; for, in my leisure moments, and sometimes when madame permitted me to go out, I would go to the house of Nicault, one of my countrymen, who is a coppersmith, and I worked with him for a recreation. Ah! well, now I will work in earnest, and with what courage."

"Ah! this is too much!" cried Madame de Varonne. "Good Ambrose, in what a sad condition fate has placed you!"

"I am content with it" replied Ambrose, "if madame can become reconciled to her change of position."

"Your attachment, Ambrose, ought to console me for everything. But to see you suffer for me!"

"Suffer when working! when you labor, you become useful, such sufferings will make me very happy. From to-morrow I commence to work. Nicault, who is a good man, will not let me want for it. He is established in St. Germain, with a good credit, and he is now in need of a good workman. I am strong, I can do well the work of two, and all will be for the best."

Madame de Varonne, not being able to find words with which to testify her admiration, raised her eyes to heaven, and could only reply with tears.

The next day the cook and the maid were discharged. Ambrose rented, in St. Germain, a clean little room, very light, and on the third floor; he furnished it with a few pieces of furniture, which belonged to his mistress, and then conducted

Madame de Varonne to it. She found there a
good bed, a large and very comfortable arm-chair,
a little table, with a writing-desk, and some paper,
above which her books were arranged upon five
or six shelves; a large wardrobe, which contained
her linen, her dresses, and a quantity of thread,
with which to work; a silver spoon, for Ambrose
did not wish that she should eat with pewter;
and the little purse which contained the thirty
louis d'or.—(a gold coin used in France, equal in
value to about four dollars in American money or
United States currency.) In a corner of the
room, behind a curtain, was concealed the little
earthenware, which was to serve as the kitchen
for Madame de Varonne.

"There is," said Ambrose, "all that I have
been able to find that is good for the price that
madame wished to give for her lodging. There
is only one room; but the servant will sleep on a
mattress, rolled under Madame's bed."

"How! the servant?" interrupted Madame de
Varonne.

"Pardon! Could madame do without a servant
to make her soup, to attend to her errands, and
to undress her?"

"But, my dear Ambrose—"

"Oh! this servant will not cost you much: she
is only a child of thirteen years of age; you will

not give her any wages, and she will always stay with Madame. As for me, I have made arrangements with Nicault. I told him that I was included in the retrenchment that madame was obliged to make; that I was in need, and asked nothing better than work. Nicault, who is rich, and, more than that, a good man, lets me sleep in his house; it is only two steps from here; he will feed me, and give me twenty cents a day. Living is cheap at St. Germain; so, with twenty cents a day, madame will be able to live easily, as she will have some provisions and a little money left: I did not wish to say all this before the little Suzanna, your new servant. Now I am going to look for her."

Ambrose went out immediately, and returned in a moment after, holding by the hand a pretty little girl, whom he presented to Madame de Varonne:

"This is the young girl of whom I have had the honor to speak to madame. Her father and mother are poor, but industrious; they have six children, and madame will do a very good action in taking this one in her service."

After this preamble, Ambrose, in a severe tone, exhorted Suzanna to behave well; at last he bade good-bye to Madame de Varonne, and went to the house of his friend Nicault.

Who could tell all that passed at the bottom of Madame de Varonne's soul? She was filled with gratitude and admiration, and could not recover from the surprise that she experienced from the sudden change in the manners and in the disposition of Ambrose.

This man, always so abrupt, so coarse, appeared no more the same; since he became her benefactor, he was only more grateful; he united to the most considerate behavior the delicacy of heroism, and his heart had learned, in one moment, the tenderness and respect that we should always show to the unfortunate. You saw that he felt how sacred are the obligations that our own good deeds impose upon us, and that one is not truly generous if he humiliates, or even if he embarrasses, in the least degree, the unfortunate one that he is assisting.

The day after that upon which Madame de Varonne had taken possession of her new home, she did not see Ambrose the whole day, because he was at work; but he came in the evening for one moment, and begged Madame de Varonne to send little Suzanna upon some errand. When he found himself alone with his mistress, he drew from his pocket twenty cents, wrapped up in paper, and placing them upon the table, said, "Behold the gains of the day!"

Then, without waiting for a reply, he called Suzanna, and returned to the house of Nicault. After making such a use of his day's work, how peaceful must have been his sleep, how sweet his dreams! For this is what we experience in doing a good action. Let us judge, therefore, how inexpressible must have been the satisfaction which such an heroic action must have procured.

Ambrose, faithful to the duties that he had imposed upon himself, came every day to pay a visit to Madame de Varonne, and left with her the reward of his day's work. He only reserved, at the end of each month, as much money as was necessary to pay for his washing; and what he spent on Sunday for some beer, he asked of Madame de Varonne, and received it as a gift.

In vain Madame de Varonne afflicted with thus robbing the generous Ambrose, wished to persuade him that she could live on much less. Ambrose either would not listen to her, or appeared to understand with so much difficulty, that she was soon forced to be silent.

In hopes of inducing Ambrose to procure for himself a little more comfort, Madame de Varonne, on her part, devoted herself, almost without ceasing, to needle work, Suzanna aided her, and took out her work to sell; but when Madame de Varonne spoke to Ambrose of the profit that she was reaping from her work, he replied simply, "So much the better" and spoke of something else. Time produced no change in his conduct; during four entire years he was never seen to deviate from it for one single instant.

At last the moment approached when Madame de Varonne was to experience the most heart-rending grief. One evening, while waiting for Ambrose, as usual, she saw the servant of Nicault enter her room, who came to tell her that Ambrose was sick, and was forced to keep his bed. At this news Madame de Varonne begged the servant to lead her immediately to the house of Nicault, and at the same time she ordered Suzanna to go for a physician. Madame de Varonne, on arriving at the house of Nicault, caused much surprise to the latter, who had never seen her. She told him that she wished to go to Ambrose's room.

"But, Madame," replied Nicault, "it is impossible."

"How so?"

"It is necessary to ascend a ladder to reach this garret."

"A ladder! Ah! poor Ambrose! I beg you to lead me there."

"But, Madame, still again I tell you, you will risk breaking your neck; and then you could not stand up in Ambrose's room, it is built in such an ugly hole."

At these words Madame de Varonne could scarcely restrain her tears; and again begging Nicault to guide her, she came to the foot of a little ladder, which she ascended with difficulty, and which led her to a garret, where she found Ambrose lying on a straw-bed.

"My dear Ambrose," cried she, on seeing him, "in what a condition do I find you? And you said that your lodging pleased you, and that you were comfortable!"

Ambrose was not in a state to reply to Madame de Varonne; for almost an hour he had been unconscious. Madame de Varonne, on perceiving this, gave herself up entirely to her grief. At last, Suzanna returned with a physician. The latter, on entering the miserable lodging of Ambrose, was strangely surprised to see, near the straw-bed of a poor tinker, a well dressed lady, whose distinguished air announced high birth, and who appeared overcome with despair. He approached the sick man, examined him attentively, and said that they had sent for him when it was too late. Judge of the state of mind of Madame de Varonne, when she heard this mournful decision pronounced.

"So," said Nicault, "it is his fault, poor Ambrose: for more than eight days he had been sick, and I wished to prevent him from working; but he would have his own way. He has only remained in bed this morning, and still we had much trouble in persuading him to do so. To enter our house, he burdened himself with more work than he could do; he has killed himself with over-working."

Each word that Nicault uttered was a mortal wound for the unhappy Madame de Varonne. She advanced toward the physician, and, with clasped hands, she implored him not to leave Ambrose. The doctor had some humanity; besides his curiosity was excited in a most lively manner. He promised to pass a part of the night with Ambrose. Madame de Varonne sent to her house for some mattresses, some bed-clothes, and some linen. With them she prepared a bed for Ambrose, the physician and Nicault placing him softly upon it; then Madame de Varonne threw herself upon a wooden stool, and gave free vent to her tears. About four o'clock in the morning the physican left, after having prescribed for the sick man, and promised to return at noon. You may well imagine that Madame de Varonne did not leave Ambrose for one moment. She passed forty-eight hours at his pillow, without receiving from the physician the slightest hope. At last, on the third day, he announced that he believed he found him better, and the same evening he declared that he thought Ambrose would live.

I cannot picture to you the joy, the delight, of Madame de Varonne on seeing Ambrose out of danger. She wished to watch him again the following night, but Ambrose, who had now recovered his consciousness, was not willing to consent. She returned home, worn out with fatigue. The physician presented himself the next day at her house; he showed so much interest in her, he appeared so touched with the care that she had taken of Ambrose, that Madame de Varonne could not help replying to his questions. She satisfied his curiosity, and related to him her history.

Three days after this confidential conversation, the doctor, who did not live in St. Germain, was obliged to return to Paris; he set out hastily, leaving Ambrose in a convalescent state.

However, Madame de Varonne found herself now in a critical situation. In eight days she had spent for Ambrose the little money that she possessed; she had just enough to provide for her wants for four or five days; but then Ambrose would not be in a state to commence work again, and she shuddered to think that necessity compelled him to work, at the risk of falling ill again.

She felt the horror of her situation, and reproached herself bitterly for having accepted the assistance of the generous Ambrose.

"Without me," said she, "he would be happy; his work would have procured for him an honest living; his attachment to me has destroyed his happiness, and may cost him his life; and I,—I shall die without liquidating the debt. Repay it! And even were it possible for me to dispose events according to my will, would it be possible for me ever to liquidate it? God alone knows how to pay the sacred debt. God alone can recompense a virtue so sublime."

One evening when Madame de Varonne was deeply absorbed in these sorrowful reflections, Suzanna, all out of breath, entered her room, and told her that a beautiful lady asked to see her.

"She is mistaken, surely," replied Madame de Varonne.

"No, no; she said to me like that: Madame de Varonne, who lives here, at the house of Mr. Daviet, on the third floor." She said that from her carriage,—a carriage with four beautiful horses. I was on the door-step. "Madame," said I, "it is here." "Will you be kind enough to say to Madame de Varonne that I ask her the favor to grant me a moment's conversation?" Then up stairs I flew, heels over head.

At this moment they heard some one softly knocking at the door. Madame de Varonne rose with extreme emotion, to go and open it. A perfectly beautiful lady presented herself, with a timid and soft manner. Madame de Varonne sent Suzanna away

"I am charmed, Madame," said the stranger to her, "to announce to you that the king has just at last been informed of your situation, and that he wishes very much to repair the injustice that fortune has shown you.

"Oh! Ambrose!" cried Madame de Varonne, clasping her hands, and raising them with an expression of the most lively gratitude.

At this exclamation, the stranger could not restrain her tears; she approached Madame de Varonne, and taking her hands affectionately:

"Come, Madame" said she to her, " come to the new lodging that is prepared for you."

"Ah! Madame," interrupted Madame de Varonne, "how to explain it! but if I dared, I would asked your permission. Madame, I have a benefactor; pray suffer me, before all, to inform him."

" You have entire liberty," replied the stranger, " In the fear of fatiguing you, I do not ask to accompany you to your friend, on your mission of gratitude. I will remain here until your return, and then accompany you to your new lodgings.

Madame Varonne hastily prepared herself to make the visit to Ambrose, to inform him of her newly recovered fortune.

Arriving at the house of Nicault she quickly ascended the steps to Ambrose's sleeping room, where she found him still in a convalescent state, and much better.

"Oh! Ambrose, she exclaimed, I have come at last to return to you my debt of gratitude and to repair all your suffering." She then related to him the good fortune of the king having bestowed the pension upon her at last, the want of which she had felt so long.

"And now" said Madame Varonne, "I will take care of you my good Ambrose, my good and faithful servant."

Descending the difficult steps once more, she asked Nicault and his son to dress Ambrose and place him in the carriage. She then drove home, and from there accompanied by the lady, the beautiful lady, as little Suzanna called her, they drove to the very beautiful apartments prepared for her, and furnished in the most elegant manner. The lady had been sent as a messenger from the king to take Madame Varonne to her new home.

The king had bestowed upon her a pension of

ten thousand francs a year, with a beautiful home, so that she lived in great comfort and some elegance; but she never forgot her faithful Ambrose, who was always her first care, and to whom she always showed the most grateful remembrance.

Pamela,

or

The Happy Adoption.

Felicia, occupied only with the education of her two daughters, lived in the bosom of her amiable family, whom she loved dearly, seeing only her relations and friends. Each day she congratulated herself on her happiness. Inclined to study, gifted with a sweet and tender-hearted soul, she never knew what hatred was. There was no sacrifice that friendship had not a right to expect of her. Indeed no one despised pomp and fortune more than she did.

However, the daughters of Felicia commenced to grow out of their childhood. Camilla, the eldest, had scarcely reached her fifteenth year when her mother, on account of the situation of her affairs, found herself forced to give her in marriage.

She had no fortune to leave to her; she could only establish her by obtaining for her an advantageous position. A suitable husband offering himself for Camilla, Felicia did not dare to hesitate; but she felt no less keenly how sad it was to be obliged to marry her daughter at so tender an age. Indeed, it is the greatest misfortune for a young person of fifteen years, as it may influence the rest of her life; her education, often being unfinished, remains imperfect. Camilla, a short time after her marriage, fell dangerously ill. Anxiety, joined to watchings and sleepless nights, caused a sensible alteration in Felicia's health, which she felt a long time after the recovery of her daughter. As her lungs appeared to be affected, the doctors ordered her to drink the waters of Bristol. She was obliged then to leave her dear Camilla in Paris, in the hands of her mother-in-law, and set out for England with Natalie, her second daughter, then in her thirteenth year.

Felicia had not taken the precaution to secure for herself a house, so that, on arriving at Bristol, she could find only a disagreeable lodging, separated merely by a partition from another room occupied by an Englishwoman, who was sick, and had been confined to her bed for ten months. Felicia, who understood English perfectly, learned from her landlady that this unhappy Englishwoman was dying of consumption. She was a widow; her husband, a young man of distinguished birth, had been disinherited by his parents for having made an improper marriage, and at his death he had only been able to leave to his wife a small pension for life; a circumstance rendered still more afflicting for this unfortunate lady, as she had a daughter five years of age, who would lose, with her, mother, all means of subsistence. The landlady praised the child, whose name was Pamela, in the highest manner, and assured Felicia that a more charming child did not exist. This story imterested Felicia in a most lively manner, and the whole evening she conversed with Natalie about their unhappy neighbor and her little girl.

Felicia and Natalie occupied the same room. It was some time after they had retired; Natalie was sleeping soundly, and Felicia was beginning to dose, when a most extraordinary noise awakened her suddenly. She lent an attentive ear, and distinguished groans, which appeared to come from the room of the Englishwoman. Then recollecting that the sick woman had only the waiting-maid and nurse to attend to her, Felicia imagined that perhaps her assistance would be of some use. She rose quickly, took her night-lamp, and went out softly, so that she might not wake Natalie. She passed through a dressing-room where her maid slept; in passing, she told her not to leave Natalie, and went out. The sick woman's door was open. Felicia, hearing some words, broken by sobs, advanced trembling. Suddenly a waiting-maid, in tears, came out of the room, crying:

"It is over! she is no more!"

"O, heaven!" said Felicia, "and I ran to offer you help!"

"She has just expired," replied the waiting-maid. "Oh my God! what will become of her unhappy daughter? I have four children: how could I burden myself with this little unfortunate.?"

"Where is her daughter?" quickly interrupted Felicia.

"Alas! Madame, the poor child is not old enough to appreciate her misfortune. She scarcely knows what death is. She loved her good mother, for there never was a more tender-hearted child. See, she is sleeping sweetly near her mother, who has just breathed her last!"

"Just God! cried Felicia, "let us take away the child from a place so sorrowful."

In saying these words, Felicia hastened toward the room. In order to approach the cradle of the child, it was necessary to pass by the side of the bed of the unfortunate English woman. Felicia trembled; she fixed for an instant her eyes, filled with tears, on the inanimate corpse, then threw herself on her knees:

"O unfortunate mother!" said she, "what must have been the bitterness of your last moments! you leave your child without shelter, without help. Ah! from the depths of eternity,— I love to think so,—you still may see and hear me. I will take the care of your child; I will never let her forget her who gave her life; each day she will implore the mercy of the Supreme Being for her mother."

In finishing these words, Felicia rose and approached the cradle with the most lively emotion. A curtain concealed the child. With a trembling hand she drew it aside softly, and discovered the innocent little orphan, whose beauty and angelic and touching face she contemplated with delight. The child was sleeping soundly: at the side of the bed of her unhappy dead mother, she tasted sweetly the charms of repose. The serenity of her brow, the ingenuous expression of her whole physiognomy that a sweet smile beautified still more, the freshness and brilliancy of her complexion, formed a striking contrast to her situation.

"See," said Felicia, "how she sleeps, at what a moment and in what a place! Poor child! in vain, when you awake, will you ask for your mother; but nevertheless, another will replace her. Yes, I adopt you; you shall find in my heart the tenderness and affection of a mother. Let us go," continued Felicia, addressing herself to the waiting maid; "help me to take this cradle into my room."

The maid obeyed with joy, and the child, without awakening, was carried softly upon her little bed into Felicia's room. The young Natalie had risen; uneasy and troubled, she run to her mother, who said to her: "approach, Natalie; I bring you a second sister; come, see her, and promise me to love her."

Natalie threw herself on her knees before the cradle, in order to see the child better. Felicia related to her in a few words all that had happened to the child. Natalie wept on hearing this sad story; she looked at the little Pamela tenderly, calling her sister; she wished it was already the next day, that she might hear her speak, and embrace her a thousand times. At last it was necessary to put her to bed. Felicia could not close her eyes the whole night; but should we desire sleep when the remembrance of a good action deprives us of it?

At seven in the morning the maid entered Felicia's chamber. As soon as the shutters were opened, Pamela awoke. Felicia ran to her cradle. The child, on perceiving her, appeared surprised; she looked at her steadily, then she smiled, and extended her arms, Felicia pressed her in hers with transports of joy; she believed in sympathy, and persuaded herself that she saw the effects of it in the sweet caresses of the little Pamela, who already inspired her with an affection so tender, and she was animated by it still more. However, it was not long before Pamela asked for her mother. This name of mother affected Felicia in a most lively manner: "Your mamma," said she, "is no longer here."

At these words, Pamela burst into tears. Natalie wished to console her; "Leave her," said Felicia, "with this touching affliction. I wish to see her tears flow: think of her situation, Natalie, and you will experience the same feeling."

When Pamela was dressed, she knelt down and said her prayers aloud. Felicia started on hearing her say: "My God, please restore mamma to health!"

"Do not say that prayer any longer," said Felicia, "for your mamma suffers no more."

"She suffers no longer!" cried Pamela, "O my God! I thank thee!"

These words troubled the soul of Felicia.

"My child," said she, "say with me; my God! please make mamma happy, and let her soul rest in peace."

Pamela repeated this prayer with touching fervor. Then turning toward Felicia, and regarding her with a timid and ingenuous air: "Let me," said she, "ask God again to grant me the favor of soon permitting me to join mamma."

In finishing these words, she perceived that the eyes of Felicia were filled with tears: she rose and threw herself on her neck, weeping. At this moment they came to tell Felicia that her carriage was ready: she took the little Pamela in her arms, and, accompanied by Natalie, she entered her carriage, and set out for Bath.

Felicia did not return to Bristol until the end of fifteen days and not wishing to return again to her first lodging, she rented another house there. Each day she became more and more attached to Pamela: the angelic sweetness, the tenderness and gratitude of this child, were for her a sweet recompense.

After having passed three months at Bristol, Felicia left England and returned to France. All her family congratulated her on the adoption of the amiable Pamela. It was impossible to see her without being interested in her, or to know her without loving her. When she had reached her seventh year, Felicia instructed her herself, and related to her the history of her unhappy mother. This sad story caused Pamela to shed abundant tears; she threw herself at the feet of her benefactress, and said all that gratitude and the most touching tenderness inspired. Pamela possessed an elevated soul; when she spoke of her feelings, she no longer used the language or the expressions of childhood. One might relate a thousand charming traits of her many fine and delicate answers, a crowd of happy and touching words, that the heart alone can inspire. This lively, yet deep sensibility shed an inexpressible grace over all her actions, and gave to her sweetness a charm, which penetrated into your very soul. You might see Pamela many times before perceiving if her features were regular, or if she was beautiful, or only pretty.

One was only struck with her interesting and ingenuous physiognomy, and with the heavenly expression of her face. You could neither examine nor praise her like another. She had large brown eyes, with long, black eye lashes. One could say nothing of her eyes; they only spoke of her expression. She had all the desire to please and to oblige, which is always given to one so naturally good; she was studious, generous, obliging, sincere, as well as artless. In short, one found in her qualities and charms whose union is very rare. She possessed shrewdness, with frankness and ingenuity; she was gay and tenderhearted; mild, yet withal lively.

The only defects that Pamela possessed arose from this extreme vivacity, which, however, never caused her the slightest movement of impatience at anything that might occur, but which gave her a thoughtlessness that few children have carried farther. Pamela, much less through negligence, than through the effect of her vivacity and her thoughtlessness, lost without ceasing, all that was given to her.

When she went to walk, she took off her hat, so as to run better, and, returning to the house, always running, she would leave her hat upon the grass. After having worked, the eagerness to go and play would not permit her to gather together her thimble, her needles, her sheath, nor to lock them up: she rose quickly, the work bag, always open, falling to the ground, Pamela jumping over all, and disappearing in the twinkling of an eye.

They were charmed to see her run in the fields or in the garden; but they had forbidden her to run in the house. Pamela, with the greatest desire to obey, forgot continually this prohibition; she fell regularly two or three times a day, and left at all the doors fragments of dress and apron. At last, by dint of prayers, exhortations, and punishments, she lost insensibly a little this excess of wildness. Felicia every morning demanded an account of what she should have in her pockets and in her work-bag; and this daily examination conduced to render Pamela less thoughtless.

One morning Felicia, following this custom, examined Pamela's pockets, and did not find her scissors there. Pamela, scolded and questioned, replied that they were not lost, that she knew where they were.

"And where are they?" asked Felicia. "mamma," replied Pamela, "they are on the floor, in my sister's little room."

"How, on the floor? And why have you left them there?"

"Mamma, I was in this little room, I was wiping my nose; in drawing out my handkerchief, my scissors fell out of my pocket; at this moment I heard your bell, I ran immediately—"

"What! Without taking time to pick up your scissors?"

"Yes, mamma—to see you sooner."

"But you knew well that I should demand an account of your scissors, and that I should scold you, when I did not find them."

"Mamma, I did not think of that; I thought only of you, and of the pleasure of seeing you."

In pronouncing these words, Pamela had tears in her eyes, and blushed. Felicia looked at her steadily, with a severe air; Pamela blushed still more. This deep blushing, and the apparent untruthfulness of the story, convinced Felicia that the innocent little Pamela had just lied.

"Get out of my sight!" said she to her. "I am sure that there is not a word of truth in all that you have just told me; leave the room without replying."

Pamela, in tears, clasped her hands, and fell at the knees of Felicia, without saying a single word. Felicia only saw in this suppliant action the avowal of her fault. She repulsed her with indignation, and overwhelmed her with reproaches. Pamela, obeying the order that she had received, kept silence, and only gave expression to her grief by sobs and moans.

Felicia resided then in the country; she went out to go to church, and instead of taking Pamela, as usual, she told the maid to take her, and left hastily. Arrived at the chapel, Felicia had, in spite of herself, more than one distraction. She turned her head many times toward the door, and at last saw Pamela enter, her eyes red and tearful; the poor little one knelt down humbly on the steps of the stairway. The maid told her not to stay there with the servants, but to go forward.

"This place is yet too good for me," replied Pamela.

This humility touched Felicia: she made a sign to Pamela to approach. The poor child wept with joy, on taking her place by the side of her adopted mother.

After service was over, Felicia's maid approached her.

"Pamela," said she, "did not lie."

"How?"

"No, Madame; she begged me to go down with her into the little room, and we found there the scissors on the floor, as she said."

"Good Pamela!" cried Felica, taking her in her arms; and you let me accuse you, and treat you so ill, without saying anything in your justification?"

"My dear mamma, you had forbidden me to speak."

"And you fell at my knees; you appeared to ask pardon."

"I should always ask pardon when mamma is angry with me; when she scolds me, I am surely wrong."

"But I was unjust."

"No; my benefactress, my tender mother, can never be so with me."

Who would not love a child capable of such an attachment and who showed such sweetness, and such a touching submission?

At seven years of age, Pamela suffered much with her teeth. She had also, at this period, a languor, or sort of decline, which lasted for more than a year. Felicia, in order to take better care of her, made her always sleep in her room. Pamela, seeing the uneasiness of Felici, sought to conceal her sufferings, her long, sleepless nights. Felicia rose often, took her in her arms, and gave her something to drink. Pamela never received any of these little cares without shedding tears of tenderness and gratitude. She would always intreat Felicia to return to bed quickly.

"Sleep, mamma," she would say;"your sleep does me good. When I know by your breathing that you are asleep, I suffer a thousand times less."

There was no good or fine feeling that was a stranger to Pamela's heart, even those that ought to be the fruit of reflection and education. She scarcely remembered England; she loved Felicia too dearly not to love France; but she never forgot that she was English, and preserved for her country a most virtuous attachment. One day, when she was eight years old, Felicia was writing, and Pamela playing quietly near her. There was then war with England; suddenly Felicia heard the sound of cannon; she listened and exclaimed:

" There, perhaps that announces a victory over the English."

On saying these words, her eyes fell on Pamela, and her surprise was extreme, on seeing her face grow pale, then blush, and cast down her eyes. At this moment several persons entered the room:

they came to tell her that dinner was served. Pamela appeared trembling and troubled. Felicia, wishing to look into the depths of her soul, said to her:

"We must know why there was such a cannonading. I flatter myself yet that we have beaten the English."

Scarcely had Felicia finished these words, than Pamela, bursting into tears, threw herself at her feet.

"O mamma!" cried she, "pardon my grief! I do not love France less, but I was born in England!"

This singular feeling for one of her age touched Felicia deeply.

"My child," said she "a touching and sublime instinct inspires you better than reason could! In believing you have committed a fault, you have fulfilled a sacred duty. Preserve always for your country, and for that of your father, this tender interest! Love the French—you should do so; but never forget that England is your country."

These words animated Pamela and penetrated her with joy, and the same evening, before retiring, she added to her prayers this one:

"My God! grant that the English and French may no longer hate one another, and that they may never do each other any harm."

With such a good heart, it was impossible that Pamela should not possess a sincere and tender piety. Certain that God saw and heard her every instant of her life, she never committed any fault without asking His pardon with the most touching tears of the truest repentance. But before imploring this pardon, she accused herself to Felicia:

"Would God pardon me," said she, "if I was wanting a confidence in mamma? Besides, a fault weighs much more heavily, when mamma is ignorant of it; and then it is so sweet to open your heart to those whom you love! Mamma will give me, perhaps, a little penance; but she will speak, she will reason with me, she will praise the sincerity of her Pamela, she will embrace me a thousand times; and this evening on retiring, when I shall have asked for her blessing, she will give it with still more tenderness than usual, if it is possible."

After these reflections, Pamela threw herself into the arms of her mother, and she found there the reward of her candor and her affection.

Not wishing to be separated from her benefactress, preferring, above every other pleasure, that of being with her, even without speaking to her; established in her room, whilst Felicia read, wrote, or practised her music, Pamela would amuse

herself in silence and without making the least
noise. From time to time, however, she would
rise softly, and approaching Felicia, embrace her,
and then return to her place. More than once,
leaving her playthings suddenly, she came and
threw herself weeping into the arms of Felicia:

"Instead of playing," said she, "I was thinking
of you, mamma, and of your kindness."

In speaking thus, Pamela fell at the feet of her
benefactress; she clasped her knees, and with a
passionate expression, and all the energy of feeling and gratitude, she would recall all that she
owed to her.

Such an extraordinary child, so engaging, so
loving, necessarily could not be an ordinary person; also, Pamela, at seventeen years, fully justified all the hopes that her childhood had inspired.
She was well educated, possessed the most agreeable talent, and all that sweet address which is so
becoming to a woman. There was no kind of
needle-work that she could not do; she drew well,
painted flowers perfectly, and played on the harp
in a most superior manner; a talent so much the
more precious for her, as she owed it solely to her
mother, who had been her only teacher of the
harp. Pamela loved reading, especially natural
history and botany. She wrote well, and as to her
style, they scarcely had to form it; for with so

tender and sweet a soul, how could she write without taste, or fail in strengh and imagination? She had preserved the ingenuousness and all the graces of her childhood, caressing manners, a frank and communicative sprightliness, and that attractive sweetness which won all hearts. As the favorite amusement of her childhood had been to exercise in running and jumping, the consequence was that she enjoyed excellent health; although her features were delicate, her figure small and light, she had, notwithstanding, astonishing strength. It was impossible to exceed her in running; no one walked better, or danced with more grace. She united to all these charms a goodness that she never deviated from, and which was always the same. She often worked in secret for the poor; she merited the praise that a modern author gave to some unfortunate queen: "She displayed those sweet and benevolent virtues which *philosophy teaches* men, and which *nature gives* to women."

Natalie was seven years older than Pamela, and had been in society for some years, as well as her sister, Camilla. These two daughters made much happiness for their mother. But this pure felicity was troubled by an event which plunged Felicia in the greatest affliction:

She had a young sister-in-law named Alexandrine, who, by her virtues and her talents, was the delight of her family.

Suffering for six months with a debility which at first was not thought dangerous, Alexandrine resolved to pass a year in the southern provinces. Felicia experienced the double sorrow of seeing her mother set out with Alexandrine. This virtuous mother consented to separate from her daughter, to undergo the fatigue of a sad journey and the suffering of a long absence, to follow a daughter-in-law, to whom her care seemed to have become necessary. Alas! she carried away with her some consoling hopes, but soon lost them, never to return. The journey only increased the sufferings of Alexandrine. At last the most terrible symptoms extinguished every ray of hope.

Felicia, informed by her mother of these unhappy details, sought still to delude herself, when she received from her a letter, couched in these words:

"Nice, November 8th, 1872—

"She is still alive; but perhaps, when you receive this letter, she will be dead. O my daughter! What will become of your unhappy brother? What will become of me, with his grief and my own? And I am two hundred miles away from you! This angelic creature that we are about to lose, we have only known imperfectly. A tranquil and fortunate life, such as hers has been, could not bring out the sublime virtues that she possessed; whereas, from the darkness and obscurity of poverty, they might have shone with a great light. You have no idea of her fortitude, of her piety, of her patience, of her perfect resignation. I have told you that she deceived herself about her condition. I was in error, she was perfectly well aware of it; even on setting out from Paris, she confided it to her maid. I have the detail from Julia herself. To soften the horror of our situation, the invalid wished at last to persuade us that she preserved the illusion that we had lost; but yesterday she betrayed herself to me. We were alone; she told me that she desired to receive the sacraments the next day, and she begged me to announce it to her husband, with all the precaution and management that was necessary to prevent him from being alarmed; then she fell into a deep reverie. In order to draw her out of these sad reflections, I told her that I had written to you this morning. At these words she appeared to wish to confide something to me and I perceived that she was undecided. I pressed her hand in mine, asking her if she desired to send you some message. "Yes," she replied, "an uneasiness torments me, it is this; you know that at thirteen years of age I had the misfortune of losing my mother; they placed me then in the convent; a few days after, a poor woman who was paralyzed came and asked to speak to me in the parlor; she told me that my mother, during the two last years of her life, had supported her. I embraced this unfortunate woman, weeping; from that time I took care of her myself. Please, dear mamma, please recommend this woman to my sister, and tell her, from me, that I leave her this charge, as a token of my friendship. Julie will give you her address. Pray send it to-morrow to my sister."

"I could only reply with tears—Alexandrine kissed my hand with a most heart-rending expression. At this moment the little dog Zennire, that you remember, and that she loves so well, wished to jump upon her bed. I took it on my lap. Your sister leaned down to kiss it: "Poor Zennire!" she said, "Mamma, you love dogs, I give her to you; promise me to keep her always."

You will know, my daughter, how to appreciate such traits. At the moment of leaving us, to think of all, to forget nothing! At twenty-four years, beautiful, happy, enjoying the greatest consideration, about to be separated for ever from a husband most beloved, from a charming child, from a cherished aunt, who was at once for her a generous benefactress and a most amiable friend!

At last, in consummating the saddest sacrifice, to preserve a humanity so touching; to be occupied with a virtuous care of assuring herself of the fate of the unfortunate one of whom she had been the sole support; to bequeath to you her poor woman; again to occupy herself with little details from which even a slight illness would distract another—not even to forget the dog! Ah! who would not admire a goodness so considerate, a fortitude so heroic? Adieu, my daughter! I send you the only consolation that I can offer you at this moment: it is the address of the poor woman. To see and take care of her will bring you a sweet consolation."

As soon as Felicia had read this letter, she sent for her carriage, and, accompanied by Pamela, she set out for the Faubourg St. Jacques. It was there that the poor woman lived, who was called Madame Busca, and who in that quarter, went by the name of *the holy woman.* The astonishment that Felicia and Pamela experienced, on seeing her, and listening to her, was only equal to the pity with which she inspired them. This unfortunate paralytic had her feet and hands entirely withered and shrivelled. Her fingers, horribly elongated, appeared dislocated, and had lost all human shape. Her face showed only a hideous mass, frightfully emaciated, and of a deathlike pallor. She could neither raise nor turn her head, it rested on her breast; and in this horrible condition for seventeen years she had, however, preserved all her faculties. She was lying in a large room, neatly arranged; a clergyman, with a venerable face, was seated at the side of her bed.

Felicia, on entering, made herself known as the sister-in-law of Alexandrine. At these words the poor woman raised her eyes to heaven, and at the same time her face was covered with tears.

"Ah! Madame," cried she, "what an angel you have for a sister! She is very young, and yet for eleven years she has supplied me with every thing. If you knew, madame, what care I have received!"

"Did she come often to see you?"

"Before her marriage, as she could not go out of the convent, I was taken three times a week to her parlor; then she asked permission to pass the grating, in order to be nearer to me; she brought me breakfast that she had prepared herself. As I could not use my hands, she fed me, and with such kindness, such attention! Indeed madame, do you know the greatest punishment that her nurse could inflict upon her? It was to say: "To-morrow you shall not feed Madame Busca; it is I who will wait on her alone." Then she became as obedient as a lamb. She always honored me by calling me mother, and she wished that I should call her my daughter. Ah, well! when I saw that the nurse was not satisfied with her, I called her *Miss*. This dear child could not contain herself then: the tears would spring to her eyes, and she would immediately go and ask pardon of her nurse. You weep ladies, pursued the good woman: "What would you do if I were to tell you all that she has done for me since her marriage? A young and charming lady, as she is, to come every two or three days, and shut herself up for whole hours with a paralytic! She brought me linen, fruit, preserves, and she often read to me a chapter from the holy scriptures. You know, madame, how divinely she sings. One day I begged her to sing for me. "I only know the ugly, worldly songs which would not please my mother, but I will learn for her some beautiful hymn." In short, four or five days after, she came to sing for me several Christmas hymns of great beauty. In truth, madame, I believe I saw, I believe I heard, an angel! Another time she brought her harp, and she played for me for more than two hours. But this is not all, madame: you see the condition in which I am; you must know, still more, that all my limbs are frightfully deformed, and that I never pass a week without having the most terrible convulsions If it was not, madame, to make you better acquainted with your most estimable sister, I should not dare to enter into such details."

"Ah! speak, go on," interrupted Felicia quickly, shedding tears freely; "speak!"

"Ah, well! madame," replied the woman, "the sweet Christian humanity of this dear angel was such, that there were no services that I was not forced to accept from her. For example, since you command me, I will tell you that no one could cut my nails without causing me very great suffering, at least unless done with great dexterity: and this is the care with which she charged herself regularly. Surely, madame, you must have remarked how white and delicate were her little hands; but you are ignorant that every week these pretty hands washed the feet of a poor, infirm woman."

The woman was silent, and her tears commenced to flow. Felicia and Pamela were not able to speak. There was a moment of deep silence. At the expiration of a few moments, a young girl entered the room, and asked the poor woman if she wanted anything. The woman thanked her, and the young girl went out. Then the clergyman, who remained seated at the head of the woman's bed, addressed himself to Felicia:

"Madame," said he, "will learn surely with interest that this young person who offered her services to Madame Busca, is the daughter of one of her neighbors, and all the other neighbors of Madame Busca are as obliging. One comes to work for her, another arranges her room, a third charges herself with bringing her light, and lighting her fire; in short, madame, the spirit of charity of your estimable sister seems to animate every one who inhabits this house. It is true that the example of this young and virtuous lady has contributed not a little to increase the activity of a zeal so laudable."

"Ah!" said Felicia, "with what admiration I feel myself penetrated!"

"Indeed, Madame," replied the clergyman, "what you have just heard, with this poor woman before you, merits well to inspire you with such sentiments. If you could know, madame, This unfortunate woman! Her piety, and the sublimity of her religion! She has not described to you all her misfortunes: this withered and immovable body is covered with sores and ulcers. I spare your feelings the details that you could not hear without shuddering."

"Ah! the unfortunate one!" cried Felicia, "What! Could no one relieve her sufferings? Is there no remedy?"

"No, madame, there is no human art that can

relieve them; but she is so much the more admirable, that she never finds anything to complain of."

"Can it be?"

"Yes, madame," replied the woman "not only do I accept these misfortunes with resignation, but I endure them with joy. Ah! how can one be astonished at that? For the sufferings of a moment, supported with patience, will obtain an eternal happiness. Our reward will be proportioned to our merits. What gratitude I owe to God for having placed me in a situation where I can have a continual merit in His eyes: that of suffering without complaint: in a situation where nothing can distract me from Him; where everything invites me to occupy myself only with eternity! Oh! how dear my misfortunes are to me! They have expiated the faults of my youth, they have purified my heart, they have detached me from all the false goods of this world. The world exists no longer for me; it can no longer seduce or corrupt me, my soul no longer inhabits this strange land; it is already invited to its Creator. My God! I see Thee, I hear Thy paternal voice; it raises me, it fortifies me, it orders me to submit without murmuring; it promises me the price of an immortal crown. O my God! I obey Thee with transport, I adore Thy decrees, I bless my destiny, and I would not change it for the most brilliant fate in the universe."

In speaking thus, this woman expressed herself with as much strength as feeling; the sound of her voice no longer announced a condition of weakness and exhaustion, or one reduced by sufferings; her eyes opened and shone brightly at this moment, with an extraordinary fire. Felicia and Pamela listened and looked at her with delight.

"Ah! well! madame," said the clergyman, "would you have believed it possible that, in such a condition, you could find anyone so happy? This woman, who blesses her destiny, what would become of her without religion? What would be the horror of her situation, if she could doubt the eternal truths with which she is penetrated? The atheist who seeks to make proselytes, what could he reply to this woman, when she would say to him: You wish to snatch away from me the only consolation that remains for me, and that I can enjoy; you wish to plunge me into the most frightful despair. Cruel being! behold my misfortunes, see my fortitude, my patience, my resignation, the calmness of my soul, and shudder at your bold attempt?"

Felicia admired the justice of this reflection, and left the poor woman, promising faithfully to return to see her as often as her occupations and duties would permit her to do so. Felicia and Pamela conversed together the rest of the day about Alexandrine and the holy woman.

"How can it be," said Pamela, "that my aunt has never spoken to you of this woman?"

"It is this," replied Felicia, "which ought to fill us with admiration. Such is the character of true virtue. When reason alone causes us to perform a good action, then we are tempted to feel proud of the efforts that it has cost us; but, when it is the grace of God which inspires us to do good, instead of admiring ourselves, we say: "I do not merit any praise; I have only followed the inspirations of my heart." Have you ever seen a miser who decided to make a present? It is always bestowed with a pomp and an emphasis which proves that he is not familiar with good deeds, and consequently how much vanity he draws from them. Indeed, it costs them so much, that one is forced to pardon the foolish pride that they display. Observe, on the contrary, with what noble simplicity a generous person knows how to give. It is thus that common souls draw vanity from their good actions, because they find them so painful, that they attach to them an extreme merit; whilst great souls are preserved from this pride by their elevation, as well at their sublime inspiration for all that is good and virtuous."

" This reflection," said Pamela, "should make us love modesty very much, or at least enable those who are wanting in it to conceal their pride with care, and never to boast of any praise-worthy action, since a different course only reveals the smallness of their soul, and their want of taste for virtue."

A few days after this conversation, Felicia received the overwhelming news of the death of her sister-in-law; she had always loved her tenderly, and the details related by the holy woman had rendered her still more dear. Although she had been prepared for three months for this event, she experienced a deep grief. She hastened to find the holy woman, to taste the sorrowful consolation of weeping with her, and of listening to the sorrowful praises of the one who was the object of them.

Pamela wished to take the place of the interesting and virtuous Alexandrine, near the poor woman. She rendered the same cares, and visited her twice a week. For nearly a year she had fulfilled these touching duties, when one morning, whilst she was washing the feet of the holy woman, the door of the room opened suddenly. A man of fifty years of age, with a noble and imposing face, appeared; after having taken some steps, he stopped. Pamela was on her knees: she held the withered limbs of the poor woman, and was wiping them. In this attitude, she held her head bent down; and her long hair, falling over her face, concealed it partly. Hearing the noise that the stranger made, she raised her head, and could not restrain a movement of surprise; a virtuous blush spread over her face, and rendered her still more interesting. Turning toward an English maid who accompanied her, she scolded her a little in English for having forgotten to bolt the door.

Immediately the stranger, with delight, exclaimed in English:

"Thank heaven, this angel is a fellow countrywoman!"

The astonishment of Pamela was extreme, and her embarrassment increased still more, when she saw the stranger approach, take a chair, and seat himself gravely opposite to her. Whilst she hastened to wrap up the limbs of the good woman, before going, the stranger did not cease gazing steadily at Pamela. He was so much absorbed in his reverie, that he did not seem to perceive the embarrassment that his presence caused her. At last Pamela rose, bade adieu to the old woman, and passing before the stranger and bowing, she went out hastily.

Some days after this adventure, Pamela learned from her protegeé that the stranger had remained afterward for an hour with her; that he had asked a thousand questions about the young person that he had first seen with her; that he had asked her name, and that of the person who had brought her up.

The same evening Felicia received a letter that she read to Pamela, and which was expressed in these words:

"Madame, I have resolved not to return to England without finding out the generous person who has been pleased to adopt an English orphan. The amiable Pamela does too much honor to her country; and to the education that she owes to you, madame, not to inspire with the most lively interest an Englishmen who was not unworthy to enjoy the happiness of contemplating her virtue. I am fifty years old; so, madame, I have the right to tell you, without hesitation, that the scene which I witnessed a few days ago has made the deepest impression upon my heart.

The charming Pamela, on her knees, washing the feet of this unfortunate paralytic, will never be effaced from my memory. They told me that she had relations in England who refused to recognize her. Pray confide to me the secret of her birth. I offer you, in her behalf, the services and the zeal of the most tender father.

"I am, with respect,
' "Charles Aresly.'

"I beg you, mamma," cried Pamela, after having read this letter, "not to see this Englishman. You are every thing to me; do not seek to force the recognition of me by relations who have abandoned me. I belong to you: what, then, is wanting for my happiness?"

"But, my child," replied Felicia, "if your parents would recognize you, you would have a name, an estate."

"You give me the sweet name of daughter; you permit me to consecrate my life to you; what more could I possibly desire?"

"Let me," said Felicia, "receive this good Englishman; his admiration for my Pamela gives me, I confess it, the desire of becoming acquainted with him. He knows how to appreciate my child: is not that a claim upon me? But I promise you never to confide to him your name, without your consent."

On this condition Pamela gave her consent to the visit of the Englishman, and the next day Mr. Aresley was received by Felicia.

After the first compliments, Mr. Aresley renewed his offers to be of service, and implored Felicia to confide to him the name of Pamela's family. Felicia confessed frankly to him that Pamela herself was opposed to this confidence.

"I shall lose," said Mr. Aresley," "the opportunity of making myself useful to her."

"At least, Sir," replied Pamela, "do not doubt my gratitude. I cannot look at the least change in my fate without fear, since I find in the tenderness of my generous benefactress a felicity which fills all the desires of my heart; but I am not the less touched by your kindness."

Mr. Aresley looked at Pamela with emotion, and turning toward Felicia:

"I set out," said he, "at the end of this week; may I dare to hope, Madame, that you will permit me to recall myself sometimes to your remembrance?" Felicia thanked him, and asked for his address.

"I no longer live in London," said Mr. Aresley, "and I often travel; but if you will, Madame, address your letters to London, to the care of Mrs. Selwin, they will surely reach me.

At the name of Selwin, Felicia seemed excited, and Pamela troubled. Mr. Aresley, who was looking at Felicia, remarked her surprise, and asked if Mrs. Selwin had the pleasure of being acquainted with her.

"I am acquainted with her name," replied Felicia.

"This name," replied Mr. Aresley "is mine."

"Indeed!"

"Yes, Madame; I renounced it on marriage, in order to obtain a property that I could not possess without taking the name of the family. I have been a widower for ten years, and I have no child."

"Had you a brother?" asked Felicia with extreme emotion.

"Alas! Madame," replied Mr. Aresley," "I have had two, and I lost them. Mrs. Selwin is the widow of the second; and the third—"

"Well, Sir?"

"This unhappy one, carried away by a sad passion, did not recognize the paternal authority; he was disinherited. Repentance and grief shortened his days; our unfortunate father followed him quickly to the tomb. I was absent then: a new series of misfortunes forced me to prolong my journey, and I only returned to England at the end of four years. I learned there the death of the widow of my second brother. She had left a daughter: I formed the project of looking for this child, and adopting her. The woman who took care of her had just died; but the husband of this woman told me that he believed that the unfortunate orphan only survived her mother a few months. This man added that he did not see his wife until six months after the death of my sister-in-law, and that then the child was no longer alive."

On pronouncing these words, Mr. Aresley perceived that Pamela sought in vain to conceal the tears with which her face was bathed. Surprised at her agitation, at her paleness, he looked at her with emotion. Felicia, as troubled as Pamela, held one of her hands in hers, and pressed this trembling hand tenderly.

Suddenly Pamela, quite distracted, rose, and advancing with a trembling step toward Mr. Aresley:

"Yes," said she, "I ought to know the brother of my father."

"Great Heavens!" exclaimed Mr. Aresly, springing toward her.

Pamela, seized with a fear that she could not conquer, receded, and threw herself into the arms of Felicia.

"O my mother!," said she, in tears, "my benefactress, it is to you alone that I belong; keep your child: do not abandon her. If you give up your right to me, you will kill me.

In finishing these words, Pamela allowed her head to fall upon Felicia's bosom : her eyes closed, she fainted. Felicia, beside herself, called for assistance. Pamela soon recovered her consciousness, and opened her eyes. Mr. Aresley seized one of her hands.

"O Pamela!" said he to her, "banish all these foolish fears, which insult me. I have neither the right nor the inhuman desire to tear you away from the arms of your adopted mother; you should consecrate to her every moment of your life. If truly you are that child, that unfortunate Selwin, that I have for so long a time deplored as lost, you will only find in me a friend, a tender father, incapable of exacting from you the slightest sacrifice."

Pamela threw herself into the arms of Filicia; she expressed her joy and her gratitude to Mr. Aresley with that grace, that passionate emotion, that characterized her. Felicia hastened to seek a casket which contained the proofs of the birth of Pamela. Mr. Aresley found there some letters and papers that Mrs. Selwin's maid had formerly remitted to Felicia.

This woman having received then some presents from Felicia, they easily supposed that, in order not to share them with her husband, she had reported the death of the young Selwin, feeling sure that this child would never appear again in England.

Mr. Aresley, seeing his wishes all consummated, on finding that his niece was the same young person whose virtues had made such a deep impression on his heart, wished that she should take her own name from that day; and, from that time, his affection for Pamela became so tender, that he established himself in France, to be near her. Pamela knew well how to merit his benefits, by her attachment and gratitude. She never left Felicia; and her first care, the sweetest of her duties, was always to render her perfectly happy.

Punctuality.

Antoinette and her brother Eugene, were two pretty, bright, sprightly children, who with their parents Madame Lavalle and her husband lived in Paris, and occupied a beautiful "appartment," as they are called there, (which means an entire floor) opposite the Champs Elysee, which is one of the most beautiful parks in Paris. Here, from their windows they looked out upon these lovely grounds, where well-dressed, gay people were driving, laughing and talking, where the trees were grand, and the flowers beautiful, and everything most charming.

Antoinette, or Nettie as they called her at home, was a very engaging little girl of thirteen; bright, and sparkling, studious when she was not playing, amiable and affectionate, generous and graceful; what more could she possess, I hear you say, and you think she was faultless? wait! and you shall decide.

It is true she might have been more intelligent looking, if she had not been compelled to wear her hair banged, which entirely hid her forehead, that most intelligent portion of the human face; but it was fashionable to have the hair banged, and Dame Fashion is inexorable, and Madame Lavalle was very punctillious with regard to etiquette and fashion, the latter of which, when carried to excess is remarkably silly. Her eyes which were pretty brown eyes, always looked as though they were looking out from a thicket. Antoinette had in my estimation one very deplorable fault; it is true the world generally is very lenient with such a fault, and scarcely considers it an imperfection. She was never punctual; she was never ready in time to go anywhere; she never rose in time, she was never punctual at meals, she was never in time for school, always tardy, always behind, always running after time, instead of taking it by the "forelock."

Unfortunately for Nettie, her mama did not set a very good example, for Madame Lavalle considered it quite vulgar to be punctual, indeed I am very sure that I have heard her express an opinion to that effect. So that Nettie was allowed to carelessly fall into this bad habit, which is so deplorable in its results, and which leads to so many mistakes.

One very bright day the carriage drove up as usual for Madame Lavalle's morning drive. Madame never went to dress, untill she saw the carriage, or heard that it was there; consequently the horses were kept waiting, and became restive, and the coachman grumbled, and all things were not as serene, as if she had been punctual. When at last, however, Madame Lavalle was dressed and seated in the carriage, Nettie, as usual, was not ready.

"Where is Nettie", said Madame Lavalle, "not ready?" I will not wait." So the carriage drove off, and Nettie was left, to her great disgust, when she came down at last, and found that her mama had drivee away.

"Too bad!" exclaimed Nettie, "such a lovely morning for a drive." "Next time I certainly will be dressed in time." But a child's disappointment and grief are short-lived, and their sorrows are like april skies, only over cast for a little while, when the unclouded blue appears again. The day was charming, and she soon found herself in the Champs Elysee playing with the children. Her Uncle Col. Xavier Leblanc, who was also amusing himself with a quiet stroll through the Park, saw Nettie, and called to her.

"What is the matter little one, that you are not with mama driving?"

"I was too late," replied Nettie, "and mama could not wait."

"Toujours tarde" said her uncle "always late" "Truly thou dost think that time will wait for thee. Time and Tide wait for no man, not even for a pretty little girl like you Nettie. I fear you will be late even on your wedding day." "Eh! bien, so goes the world—I think sometimes, he said to himself, that it is upside down, people are so careless. Here is my sister, bringing up this child with no regard for time. She should be taught that time waits for no one, that there is a time for every thing etc, and he repeated over, all the old sayings about time down from the primer; and then there is a time to die, he said almost unconsciously, ah! well, that is a gruesome thought certainly, on this bright morning;" and he took out his gold snuff box set with diamonds, and took two or three pinches, then settling his eye glasses firmly on his prominent nose, and taking his gold-headed cane, proceeded on his morning promenade. Ah! walk on Col. Xavier Leblanc. How many of us are ready when the pale rider comes? How many of us are ready when the Angel of Death hovers over us, and the world is receding? We should not be too late then; we should be ready, our consciences, and all accounts settled; our house cleaned and set in order; our lamps trimmed, and we, ready to receive the always unwelcome guest, and to take the last journey.

Antoinette had a very dear aunt, who was a religieuse in the Convent of the Sacred Heart in Paris; a Madame da Costa; she was a very saintly religieuse, and did an immense amount of good, by the advice and council, that she gave to the young worldlings who flocked to her for guidance in their labyrinth of folly. Antoinette loved to visit her dear Tanta as she called her, but as she was never allowed to go into the streets by herself, she was always compelled to coax one of the maids to take her. Madame Lavalle's own especial maid seldom had time to attend to Nettie, so that it generally fell to the lot of old Julia the house-maid to take care of the little girl. Julie was very fond of her "*petit pigeon*," as she called her little darling, and said, that if she wished to go to the gloomy Convent, that she should go, though for her part, she would rather gossip with old Sebastian the porter, who knew every carriage and livery on the Boulevard, and the pedigree of all the occupents of said carriages; and it is a great deal to know all that, and he knows all about the silver and jewels too said Julie—think of that!"

"Oh! what nonsense," said Antoinette, "and

how can you say the Convent is gloomy? "why," continued Nettie, "Tanta is so sweet and lovely that I am never tired when I am listening to her; and her eyes shine so beautifully, like the sanctuary lamp, that they seem to light up the whole room. Oh! Julie," continued Nettie, "she tells me so many lovely ways of doing and being good, that I am sure I shall learn to be *tres sage*, after a while."

"Ah! you are good now, my pet," said old Julie, only—one thing—you are never in time. How is it *petit pigeon*, that you are always behind time? If old Sebastian was not to open the door just at the click of the minute that the bell rang, he would be discharged; and if I were not up in the morning the moment the clock struck six—*I* would be discharged too."

"I have heard mama say," said Antoinette, "that time was only made for slaves and servants."

"Hum,—Hum," mumbled old Julia, fine talk for children to hear—I declare the rich think the world was made for them; but here we are little one, and now you will see your dear aunt, and many a good lesson may she teach you."

Arrived at the Convent du Sacré Cœur, an immense and imposing looking building, Julie rang the bell, and a sister opening the door, led Antoinette at once to the parlor, to her aunt, while Julie was entertained by the sisters in the garden.

Madame da Costa folded little Antoinette in her arms, she was very fond of her sisters children, and Nettie especially.

"How art thou dear one? It has been many days since thou wert here?"

"I know it darling Tanta, but no one had time to bring me." You know how much I desire to be with you always."

"True, the world has many, demands many duties of its votaries."

"Have you made any good resolutions Nettie, since I saw you? "Have you overcome any fault? Let me see, which is the pet fault, the one that still lingers with you?

"Oh! dear Tanta, it is the same old fault, you know—I am never in time, never ready."

"Do try *cherie*, to overcome that imperfection; with that fault following you every where, you will never accomplish any thing; it will prevent you from ever making one step forward in progress, because, you will always be taking one step backward every time."

"Try to live by rule Nettie dear, it is quite as necessary, for those in the world, as for the religieuse; to live by rule, will make all things easy for you, without it, all will be confusion."

"Try to be punctual, without punctuality, you will ever be running after lost time, to try and make it up. And at the end of life, you have nothing to look back upon, but a series of mistakes, and failures, caused by this want of *punctuality*."

"I consider it," continued Madame da Costa, "as one of the greatest evils in life. In the absence of punctuality, you become indolent. People do not like te be punctual, because it involves a certain amount of exertion, and they are too indolent to make it. You do nothing at the right time, consequently there is much left undone. If you are not punctual, you are not generally exact; and from being inacurate, in even the most minute matters, you are very apt to become untruthful. This is perhaps a gloomy view to take of it, but you must remember dear one, that each time you are not ready, that you are not punctual, that you take a step backward, and you should try each day to take a step *forward*, one step toward perfection.

One day, perhaps, dear Nettie, you may be called upon to be the head of a family, and unless you then possess, order, system, regularity and punctuality, you will not succeed in making a happy, well—regulated Home."

"Darling Tanta," cried Nettie, every word that

you have uttered has dropped down into my heart, and let us hope they will bring forth blossoms and fruit."

"Try dear little one," said Madame da Costa, kissing Nettie on both cheeks, to overcome this defect, and to practise punctuality daily. Believe me, it is one of the great *secrets of success*. And now, dear child, adieu for a little while, and may the Angels of peace and order attend thee."

Madame da Costa then rang the bell, and Julie appeared to lead Antoinette Home.

Nettie was silent and meditative on her way Home, she scarcely spoke to old Julie, who jogged along grumbling, for her *petit pigeon* generally amused her, with her prattle; but Nettie was treasuring up the precious pearls of wisdom, that had fallen from the sweet lips of her saintly aunt, and she was pondering on all these reflections in her heart, and making many good resolutions.

"Tomorrow I will begin," said Nettie half out loud,—

"What is that,.?" said Julie, who heard something, and wanted to talk. "What are you going to do tomorrow?"

"I am going to rise at six, as you do Julie, and then I will be sure to be ready for breakfast."

"Ah! Dieu; cried the old woman, why little one, you will be sleepy all day."

"No, no, I will not, it will give me plenty of time to dress and say my prayers, and to take a run in the garden, and then, be in time for breakfast; and then I will not be late at school, and I shall keep up, and be punctual all day."

"You had better stay in bed two hours longer," said Julie, "I know that I would not get up, if I was not forced to."

"No, no, said Antoinette, I will commence tomorrow; Tanta has often told me, never to put off."

"Well, well, said Julie, I expect you will be a little Saint soon, and now here we are at Home, and I must have a chat with Sabastian."

Dinner was served; The lights were lighted; The table beautifully decorated with flowers; and as Madame Lavalle entered one door, Antoinette entered the other.

Her mama exclaimed,—"why Nettie! are you really in time for dinner; under what good spell are you resting, that such a reformation has taken place?"

"Oh! dear mama, I have spent the afternoon with Tanta, and she has said such lovely things; I am really now, going to try and overcome that hateful fault, of always being behind time: you shall see mama, I will be in time for breakfast, and for school, and ready to drive with you."

"Now verrons," said Madame Lavalle, "I hope so."

True to her word, Nettie was up at six the next morning. When dressed, she roamed through the Garden, and gathered lovely bouquets, for mama, papa, and Eugene, and placed them beside their plates.

Papa came in, pinched her ear, and said "what an early bird." Mama entered, and looked pleased, and Eugene exclaimed, "why Nettie, what is the matter? you are turning over a new leaf."

Nettie found a great satisfaction in being praised, and in pleasing others, and finally felt very much pleased with herself. The effort to overcome this fault, and be really good, was such a healthy moral exercise, that it acted like a tonic, and braced her for future exertion. Nettie really was in earnest. We so often have the most beautiful *intentions*, so lovely, that they might be called inspirations; and though we enjoy them for the time being, yet we put off putting them into practice, until the next day, and then, until a more convenient season; and then a feeling of indolence comes over us, and we do not feel like making any exertion, and put it off still farther; until we forget that we have ever had a *good intention*.

His satanic majesty loves dearly such indolent natures, such procrastinating souls, that so often fall a prey, to his wiles and temptations. While activity, energy, industry and Zeal, in well directed efforts for some good end, are really the most invincible armor, that we can put on, in self defense.

Yes, Nettie was in earnest! she was fully aware of her fault, and most determined to conquer.

For the afternoon drive, she was ready to accompany her mother, and in driving through the Boulevard, they met Col. Xavier Leblanc, who accosted them gaily. "Why, little one, were you really ready to drive to-day?"

"Oh! yes," replied Madame Lavalle, Nettie has turned over a new leaf, and I have great hopes of having a most exemplary daughter."

"Well!" said the Col., "I said the other day Nettie, that you would not be ready on your wedding day; but now, I say, that if you overcome that terrible fault, that is so destructive to order, peace and happiness; that I will give you on your wedding day, fifty thousand Louis d'or—that is a promise.

Nettie smiled, such promises were nothing to her,—she was working now in a good cause, to overcome nature and self. Her visits to her dear Tanta, only served to renew her efforts, which were crowned with success. Her dear aunt's prayers, together with her own exertions, served to mould her into a very brave, true woman, who learned by practise, self control, and who remembered the saintly advice of her dear aunt. "*Live by rule*" it is as necessary in the world, as in a religious life. When she grew up to womanhood, she was the model for her young companions; and when later she formed a marriage with a most estimable gentleman, and became the mother of many sweet children; she was like the wise woman in Proverbs, "her children and husband rose up and called her blessed."

Punctuality was the watchword in her household, and order reigned supreme in her Home. For you see—*Nettie had conquered.*

www.ingramcontent.com/pod-product-compliance
Lightning Source LLC
Chambersburg PA
CBHW032156160426
43197CB00008B/941